OPEN LOOK™
GRAPHICAL USER INTERFACE
APPLICATION STYLE GUIDELINES

Sun Microsystems, Inc.

Addison-Wesley Publishing Company, Inc.
Reading, Massachusetts ■ Menlo Park, California ■ New York
Don Mills, Ontario ■ Wokingham, England ■ Amsterdam
Bonn ■ Sydney ■ Singapore ■ Tokyo ■ Madrid ■ San Juan

The OPEN LOOK Graphical User Interface was developed by Sun Microsystems, Inc. for its users and licensees. Sun acknowledges the pioneering efforts of Xerox in researching and developing the concept of visual or graphical user interfaces for the computer industry. Sun holds a non-exclusive license from Xerox to the Xerox Graphical User Interface, which license also covers Sun's licensees.

The Sun logo is a registered trademark of Sun Microsystems, Inc.
UNIX is a registered trademark of AT&T.
OPEN LOOK is a trademark of AT&T.
PostScript is a registered trademark of Adobe Systems, Inc.
Patent Pending.

Library of Congress Cataloging-in-Publication Data
OPEN LOOK graphical user interface application style guidelines / Sun
   Microsystems, Inc.
        p.   cm.
     Includes bibliographical references to (p.).
     ISBN 0-201-52364-7
     1. User interfaces (Computer systems) 2. Windows (Computer
   programs) 3. OPEN LOOK (Computer program) I. Sun Microsystems.
   QA76.9.U83063   1989
   005.4'3—dc20   89-28819
                        CIP

Sponsoring Editor: Carole McClendon
Cover Design: Hannus Design Associates
Text Design: Joyce C. Weston
Set in 11-point Helvetica Light by Inprint, Inc.

CDEFGHIJ-AL-93210
Third Printing, June 1990

CONTENTS

OPEN LOOK Graphical User Interface Application Style Guidelines

ACKNOWLEDGMENTS

The OPEN LOOK UI was developed by Sun Microsystems in partnership with AT&T. It is based on the pioneering work done on graphical user interfaces at Xerox PARC in the 1970s.

Many people at Sun, AT&T, Xerox, and elsewhere contributed over a two-year period to the design, review, implementation, testing, and refinement of the OPEN LOOK UI.

The "simple, consistent, and efficient" paradigm and many of the visual and functional guidelines for this book are based on the work of Norm Cox and Alan Mandler, members of the OPEN LOOK UI design team. Additional examples draw on the experience of application developers at Sun and AT&T. Special thanks go to Leif Samuelsson for extensive prototyping work and design contributions, and to Bev Harrison for administrative support.

Janice Winsor wrote this book. Alan Mandler provided the guidelines, illustrations, and examples, and contributed to the conceptual and organizational framework. Dan Shafer and Tony Hoeber contributed to earlier drafts. The cover design is based on artwork provided by Norm Cox.

Sun would particularly like to acknowledge the following people for their contributions:

From AT&T, Don Alecci, Bruce Barnett, Jim Cunningham, Betty Dall, Lee Davenport, George Derby, Jim Farber, Scott Hansen, Ross Hilbert, Steve Humphrey, John M. Jones, Ruth Klein, Sivan Mahadevan, Don McGovern, Marcel Meth, Carol Nelson, Marcia Paisner, Bill Sherman, Sarah Siegel, Valerie Mitchell-Stevens, Rich Smolucha, Don Ursem, and Mike Zanchelli.

From Sun, Richard Berger, AmyJo Bilson, Lin Brown, Amy Christen, David Goldberg, Steve Goldner, Tony Hoeber, Jon Kannegaard, Martin Knutson, Karen Lusardi, Henry McGilton, Mem, Richard Probst, Scott Rautmann, Scott Ritchie, Jeff Rulifson, Nannette Simpson, Ian Wallis, Bob Watson, Dianna Yee, and Geri Younggren.

From Xerox, Dave Curbow, David Jones, Janie Phillips, and Paulien Strijland.

From Addison-Wesley: Carole McClendon, Joanne Clapp, Steve Stansel, Diane Freed, and Rachel Guichard.

From Inprint, Ed Rose.

About This Book

Audience

This book is addressed specifically to designers of applications using the OPEN LOOK™ Graphical User Interface, although much of the material is of interest to anyone concerned with computers and user interface design. The "you" in this book is you in your present or future capacity as an OPEN LOOK UI application designer.

This book does not describe the look and feel of the complete OPEN LOOK UI. It assumes a basic familiarity with the OPEN LOOK UI. To get the complete picture, supplement the application development guidelines provided in this book with the information in the following two books:

☐ *OPEN LOOK Graphical User Interface Functional Specification*

☐ *OPEN LOOK Graphical User Interface Trademark Guide*

Although it is possible for an application developer to implement the OPEN LOOK UI "from scratch," the usual approach is for you to use a *toolkit* that has been written for a specific windowing platform. The toolkit provides a set of routines that implement the various interface elements as specified in the *OPEN LOOK Graphical User Interface Functional Specification*. You, in turn, use the routines provided by the toolkit to create and position the interface elements that you choose for your application.

If you are using an OPEN LOOK toolkit to develop your application, you will also need the toolkit documentation.

Refer to the glossary at the back of this book for a brief description of each element of the OPEN LOOK UI.

How This Book is Organized

Chapter 1, Design Principles: The principles of good application design using the OPEN LOOK UI

Chapter 2, Deciding How to Structure Your Application: Guidelines and questions providing you with a conceptual framework for organizing your application

Chapter 3, Overview of the OPEN LOOK User Interface: A brief look at the OPEN LOOK UI environment, its controls, and required window elements. If you are already familiar with the OPEN LOOK UI, you can skip this chapter

Chapter 4, Window Configuration: Guidelines for helping you decide on the overall configuration and presentation of your application, including types and numbers of windows you provide, how your application responds to resizing of windows and panes, types of scrolling in panes, and arrangement of controls in each types of window

Chapter 5, Data Entry, Selection, Manipulation: Guidelines for selection and keyboard use

Chapter 6, Choosing and Using Controls: Guidelines for choosing controls for the base window and other parts of your application and review of the visual feedback for controls

Chapter 7, **Naming and Grouping Controls:** Guidelines for choosing titles and labels and for grouping controls, including how to design compound controls

Chapter 8, **Menu Configuration:** A brief review of the types of OPEN LOOK UI menus and guidelines for designing menus

Chapter 9, **Messages:** Guidelines for providing appropriate information, status, and error message feedback to users

Chapter 10, **Using Color:** Guidelines about the effective use of color in your applications

Appendix A, Certification: Three levels of certification for the OPEN LOOK UI

Appendix B, Writing About the OPEN LOOK User Interface: Proper use of the OPEN LOOK trademark, an overview of the user interface using correct terminology, and guidelines for writing about the user interface

References: A list of reference books about user interface design and effective use of color

Glossary: An alphabetical list of terms used in this book with definitions.

Conventions Used in This Book

The following conventions are used in this book:

☐ Terms introduced for the first time are in *italic type* and are defined in the Glossary.

☐ Specific guidelines are identified with a checkbox.

☐ Illustrations of bad or inappropriate use of design elements are identified by the international symbol for "no" (a circle with a line through it).

☐ Mouse buttons are referred to by function, not by location on the mouse. For example, "Click SELECT" is used, not "Click LEFT" or "Click the first button."

☐ The names of mouse buttons are capitalized. For example, "Press SELECT."

☐ Keyboard keys have an initial capital letter. For example, "Press the Tab key."

☐ To perform certain functions, you hold down one key while you press a second key or mouse button. This combination of keystrokes is shown in the following way: "Press Ctrl/MENU."

See the *OPEN LOOK Graphical User Interface Functional Specification* for a detailed description of design elements and their functionality.

Trademark Licensing

The name "OPEN LOOK" is a trademark of AT&T. The right to use the OPEN LOOK trademark for toolkits and applications is subject to a certification procedure. AT&T offers OPEN LOOK UI trademark licensing for three levels of certification. Appendix A provides a detailed list of elements for each level of certification. The *OPEN LOOK User Graphical Interface Trademark Guide*, available from AT&T, provides information about certification requirements.

1

DESIGN PRINCIPLES

Introduction

The OPEN LOOK Graphical User Interface is a specification for the "look and feel" of a windowing environment for a multitasking computer system. The look and feel includes the types of objects users see on the screen and the basic conventions for how users work with those objects.

The OPEN LOOK UI is designed to provide a consistent user interface for a wide spectrum of applications. Users who are comfortable with one OPEN LOOK UI application then approach other applications with a built-in comfort level, and thus spend less time learning each application. Application developers can concentrate on designing the user interface for the application itself rather than on designing specific elements for a user interface.

The OPEN LOOK UI design is not dependent on any particular hardware or operating system environment. Device independence makes it easy to port applications developed using the OPEN LOOK UI. In addition, the OPEN LOOK UI design allows future development and incorporation of additional user interface standards.

The right to use the OPEN LOOK trademark is subject to a certification procedure. See Appendix A for more information.

This chapter discusses fundamentals of OPEN LOOK UI design principles.

Basic User Interface Design Principles

An application has "objects" (items that users see) and "actions" (operations performed on these objects). Often, an application has too many actions and objects to be presented at the same time. Your job as an application designer is to present both objects and actions to end users in a manner that is easily accessible. Once objects are selected and the actions are chosen, the operation must be intuitive to users.

The OPEN LOOK UI provides standard user interface elements for you to use in designing an application. These include windows that have panes for displaying objects and control areas and menus for initiating actions. The presence of these elements does not guarantee good application design; that depends on you. This book provides guidelines for presenting your applications in a tasteful and functional manner.

This section describes the principles that guided the design of the OPEN LOOK UI. These principles—simplicity, consistency, and efficiency—should also be applied to good application design. The first goal is simplicity.

Simplicity

Simplicity is the most important aspect of your application design for novice and intermittent users. Users want quick success which, in turn, gives them the impression that OPEN LOOK UI applications are easy and intuitive. This instills confidence for continued exploration of the capabilities of your product.

Good Visual Design

The first impression users gain of your application is determined by how it looks. A good visual presentation contributes to simplicity. Your product should look good and be distinctive but not too flashy. For example, an architect wants a new building to have a presence of its own but does not want it to look out of place in the surrounding environment. Users are more likely to be afraid to try an application that is visually overwhelming. If it looks complicated or too different, users will treat it with caution. To address the issue of good visual design, many companies have a graphic designer on the product team; this is a good idea when you are designing any product.

Good visual design allows users to distinguish instinctively between important elements. The OPEN LOOK UI provides a visual framework for applications that is clean and uncluttered, allowing users to focus their attention on the data presented in your application. Follow the guidelines in this book for presenting elements common to most applications to keep things simple for users of other OPEN LOOK UI applications. Be sure that the appearance of additional controls blends well with the other elements of the user interface.

Clearly Labeled Controls

Clearly labeled controls contribute to simplicity. At one time or another, each of us has been a beginning user. The rate at which we become more experienced is based on several factors, including our technical interest, need, and how frequently we use the product. In fact, some products are used so infrequently that users cannot be expected to remember how they operate. For example, a consumer tax preparation program might be used once a year. In that program, the command for calculating the tax return might be labeled "Calculate Return." If the program is designed to be used by accountants who would gain greater proficiency through repeated use and technical understanding, the same command might be labeled "Calculate." Both of these labels are simple. The former has an extra emphasis on simplicity because of the expected user audience. Both novices and experts appreciate the clarity. Neither type of user would appreciate a command that is hidden from view, with a more ambiguous label such as "Merge Schedule Form Data."

Familiar Framework

Both novices and experts benefit when an application looks like the real-world object it is meant to represent. For the consumer tax preparation application it makes sense for the data entry format to look like a tax form.

Consistency

There is never an excuse for not conveying program information clearly. Sometimes, however, operations themselves are inherently complex. The consumer tax return program, for example, would probably guide users through various stages of a standard process, presenting options along the way. In many cases, the more experienced users are, the more varied their actions.

Consistency enables users to apply previously gained knowledge to new areas without having to learn from scratch. Users can "figure out" consistent products by detecting and learning the similar patterns. They can then make inferences based on reasonable assumptions, both in that application and in other related applications.

Mouse and Keyboard Usage

This book recommends conventions for the operation of standard controls, such as mouse buttons and keyboard accelerators. Always follow such conventions. For example, the mouse buttons should operate consistently across all applications. Remapping the buttons can prove disastrous, especially because users have no way of knowing about the altered function of the button until it has already been pressed.

Users should be able to perform their tasks as automatically as most of us drive a car, without thinking about the location of the accelerator or brake pedal. Some people drive several different cars in a day. Imagine how confusing it would be if they had to remember which model of car has the accelerator on the left pedal, the brake on the right, and the clutch in the middle.

Many users operate several applications during a day. If each application defined the mouse buttons in a different way, users would need to focus too much attention on how to use them. The inconsistent pattern of mouse button usage would interfere with using each application.

Placement and Naming of Controls

This book suggests conventions for the placement and naming of controls that are common to most applications. For example, when applications follow a consistent convention for saving information, users only have to learn the process once. They know where to look for the controls related to saving and how to interpret the names of the controls. Once users have learned how to save information in one OPEN LOOK UI application, they do not need to learn a new way to save information in your application. Every time you follow a consistency guideline, as detailed in this book, you take advantage of experience that users have gained from other OPEN LOOK UI applications.

Standard Conventions

Sometimes you may have decide whether to make your application consistent with the OPEN LOOK UI guidelines or with a standard for the potential user community. When faced with such a decision, always design to user expectations. For example, users of a suite of office applications expect them to be consistent with one another. On the other hand, users of an application that emulates robotic controls for a factory may expect the application controls to look like a machine control panel. In such a case, it is still a good idea for the applicable, standard OPEN LOOK UI functions (loading, saving, printing, editing) to be consistent with those in other applications.

Some operations are "conceptually" similar to users, though the technical aspects are quite different to developers. In all cases, follow the users' conceptual model. For example, the specifics of loading a file from a file server might be different than downloading a record from a database server. However, most end users consider the concepts to be the same.

Working with Objects

The OPEN LOOK UI consistently applies the following methods of working with objects:

□ *Select-then-operate* means that users first choose (select) an object and then indicate the desired way to act on it (operate). This approach is sometimes called the "noun-verb" model because users say, in effect, "Take this object and do this action to it." For example, take this word and make it bold; take this window and close it.

□ *Direct manipulation* means that whenever possible users can move or copy selected objects by dragging them with the pointer to a new location. For example, users can select objects and drag them to new locations rather than issuing a command that relocates the object for them. Direct manipulation also includes the "drag-and-drop" model, which lets users transfer files between applications by dragging an iconic representation of a file and releasing, or dropping, it onto another application.

Both these methods of choosing and acting on objects avoid the use of *modes*. Users can do nothing outside a mode until the operation is complete or the mode is canceled. They might have to go through special steps to specify multiple objects. In contrast to modal operations, the select-then-operate and direct manipulation paradigms allow users to select one or more objects and take any appropriate or desired action. If users change their minds about the action, they can easily move on to something else without using the originally planned option.

Efficiency

An efficient application minimizes the number of steps required to perform an operation and provides users with shortcuts. Even beginning users want to perform actions with the minimum number of steps. More experienced users may explore additional shortcuts that allow them to do more things with a minimum number of steps: less mouse travel, fewer keystrokes, and less hand movement between the mouse and the keyboard.

Looking again at the example of a tax return preparation program, one user might fill in each of the forms in the manner prescribed by the program. During the process, users might switch to another tax schedule. An accountant might repeatedly switch from one schedule to another, do a few calculations, and manually move data that a casual user might never touch. An accountant using the tax program is likely to want a quick way to do these operations, and does not want to be prevented from performing operations that an occasional user might not attempt.

Progressive Disclosure

Designers of consumer appliances and stereo components have, for years, been addressing the problem of providing advanced features while not intimidating casual users. For example, stereo equipment often has complex controls hidden behind panels. The casual user might be satisfied to turn on a stereo, adjust the volume, and set the tuning without ever looking for more controls. The more sophisticated user can open the panel, expose all of the knobs, and tailor the sound in subtle ways. These advanced features do not confuse the casual user because they are hidden. More ambitious users have the minor inconvenience of opening the panel the first time, but they can leave it open for convenient future access.

Your application can use this same kind of progressive disclosure using standard elements of the OPEN LOOK UI. Pop-up menus and pop-up windows are like controls behind the panel of a stereo system. They provide you with a place to put controls that make your application more efficient to use. Users decide when it is appropriate and useful to display and use these controls.

You can also base the disclosure on appropriate usage, keeping controls out of the way until they are required and then displaying them based on actions users take that suggest a need for additional information. As an example, your application might automatically display a Print Options command window that shows the current print settings each time users choose an item that initiates a print request.

Pop-up Windows and Menus

The OPEN LOOK UI allows you to make sure that objects of immediate interest, such as data and frequently used controls, are visible. You can put other less-obvious or infrequently used controls in menus or in pop-up windows that are hidden until users need them. Beginning users will probably use the controls that they can see to perform application functions.

In addition to these controls, each pane of your application has a pop-up menu. The pop-up menu should contain the most frequently used controls for that pane. Instead of moving the pointer from the pane to the control area, choosing a control, and then moving the pointer back into the pane, users can choose controls from the pop-up menu.

Keyboard Equivalents and Accelerators

Keyboard equivalents provide a way for users to access controls without needing to switch between the keyboard and the mouse. Many keyboard equivalents involve holding down one key while pressing another. Accelerators let users press a key or sequence of keys on the keyboard or click a mouse button multiple times to perform specific menu or application functions quickly, without using a menu. The primary focus of keyboard equivalents and accelerators is efficiency. They do not replace application functionality; they supplement it. Many beginning users of word processing applications, although considered novices, eagerly embrace the presence of keyboard equivalents and accelerators that permit them to keep their hands on the keyboard.

Coexistence

Simplicity, consistency, and efficiency allow functions within OPEN LOOK UI applications to relate to one another coherently, as well as allowing users to switch easily between applications. Users can feel comfortable with the functional similarities between various applications, and can use the interface without being afraid that they will inadvertently issue a dangerous command.

The OPEN LOOK UI is designed to coexist with other popular user interfaces. Commonly accepted features are incorporated and enhanced, and several industry-standard conventions have been followed. Though it is difficult to coalesce the conventions of several popular interfaces into one, users can switch between environments easily without needing to focus too much attention on the basics of using each interface.

The OPEN LOOK UI is also designed to accommodate a wide range of hardware devices. Applications may work with various keyboards, screen sizes, resolutions, colors, and pointing devices. For example, the tax program might be installed on systems whose pointing device is a one-, two-, or three-button mouse. And, the application must function on a variety of monitors. Most of the issues related to this "device independence" are handled automatically by your OPEN LOOK UI toolkit. However, your applications must be programmed in a device-independent method (that is, written to expect logical events versus events based on particular hardware components).

2

DECIDING HOW TO STRUCTURE YOUR APPLICATION

Introduction

This chapter presents a series of questions and perspectives that you can use to formulate a conceptual framework for your application design. These questions can also help you gather specific information you need to make critical design decisions about the specific structure and design of the user interface for your application.

You are asked to consider

☐ Background and knowledge of your users

☐ What users see

☐ The primary focus of users' attention

☐ The secondary focus of users' attention

☐ Methods of effective user interaction with your application and its components

Use this material to gain a broad foundation for exploring the detailed design guidelines provided in the remainder of this book. If you are unfamiliar with the OPEN LOOK Graphical User Interface design or with specific terminology used in this book, see the Glossary. More specific information relating to these guidelines is presented in Chapters 3–10.

General Questions

1 What is the primary purpose of the application?

Keep that purpose in mind when dividing up the functions of your application. Make sure that primary operations that relate to that purpose are available in the base window, and that less important (subordinate or secondary) operations are not shown at the same level. Less important operations may belong in command windows. For example, a mail application is used for receiving, viewing, creating, and sending mail. Another function, such as searching for mail addresses, should receive less visual importance.

2 Who uses the application?

Consider who uses your application when deciding what terminology to use for the controls of your application, whether the application must conform to other frequently-used software or to a real-world object, and what users consider to be acceptable operating conditions.

3 Are your users novice, experienced, or expert?

Design labels for your controls based on the experience level of your users. Although it is never a mistake to label controls clearly, novice users might require more information before they can correctly interpret a command that is familiar to a more experienced user.

4 How frequently do users utilize the application?

a) Throughout the day

b) A couple of times a day

c) Once a day

d) Once a week

e) Once a month

f) Once a year

g) Varies from user to user

Consider frequency of use when deciding how clearly and simply you label controls and what additional functionality you provide for your application. For example, consider providing automatic backup of files for an application that is used continuously throughout the day.

5 Why will users be familiar with the application?

a) It is nearly identical to the real-world mechanism it represents.

b) It is similar to industry-standard software that already exists (and with which users might already be familiar).

c) It is so simple that anyone could use it, no matter what their previous experience.

Design your application to be consistent with users' expectations. If the application is nearly identical to a real-world mechanism, then it may operate differently from an application that is similar to other industry-standard software.

Icons

The icon that represents each closed window is an important part of application design. The icon may be the first part of your application that users see. Even more important than first impressions, however, is that users must be able to recognize and identify your icon easily when they are working with many applications. The icon acts like the label on a box, helping users infer the functions included in your application. Design the icon (or icons) for your application so that they are unique and recognizable, look related to, and do not stand out from the overall environment. The final icon images should be designed by a graphic artist.

Icon design is especially important when your application is divided into separate parts that can operate independently of one another. When an application is designed in this way, users must be able to identify quickly the icon for each part of your application so that they are not frustrated by opening the wrong window.

Thinking about how your application is represented as an icon can help you decide important aspects of how your application is designed.

1 What image represents a concept of your application's function?

2 Will users think of the application as representing a process?

In most cases, applications represent processes. If that is the case, and there is a common, well-known metaphor, use a graphic representation of the metaphor. For example, for a mailing application, most people understand a mail box as representing the act of receiving or sending mail. In an office environment, a mail tray might be more applicable.

a) What process does the application represent?

b) What recognizable image will users associate with the process?

3 Does the application create data files or other objects?

Some applications, such as clocks, do not create data files. However, most applications do create files and/or other objects, either locally or remotely on a file or database server. Users can use these objects to save and/or recall information.

When the resulting data is presented as an icon, it should appear related to the application that created it. For example, a mail application creates and receives pieces of mail. A postmarked envelope, in most people's minds, represents received mail. To carry the metaphor further, a mail application that sends plain text messages, along with files, might use a postcard to represent an ASCII-only message and an envelope to represent a message that includes an enclosure.

a) What objects does the application create?

b) What are the recognizable images?

c) Do the images look related to the actual application because the icons are visually similar or because the metaphors (for example, envelope and mail box) go together in a user's mind?

4 **Does it seem as though two or more visual images need to be represented?**

If the answer is yes, consider separating a compound application into multiple applications. For example, suppose you are developing a mail application and are considering how to present filing functions. Here are some examples of questions you might ask in designing a mail application:

a) Would you want to incorporate information about the filing function as part of the icon?

b) Is the filing function used independently of sending and receiving mail?

c) Is the filing function also used for non-mail objects?

5 **Does it seem as though several of your applications require the same icon?**

Consider combining individual applications into one, especially if users are likely to use both applications anyway. For example, an application for partitioning a disk and another application for formatting a disk might best be consolidated into a single application. List functions provided by each application to determine whether it is advisable to combine them.

6 **Are there applications that belong to the same family and that would benefit from visually related icons?**

If so, consider designing icons with a common theme. The theme could include variations of the same metaphor or a similar aesthetic style.

For example, applications from the same company could include the company logo positioned in the same location. Applications that relate to using a disk could each have an image of a disk in the icon.

a) Is the application part of a family of applications?

b) What is the common thread between these applications?

c) What is the visual representation of that association?

7 Will the application perform some of its operations while users do something else with another application?

Some applications run lengthy activities during which users might switch to another task. During those times, users might not want the application to take up much space on the workspace. At the same time, however, they might want to check the status of the task to see how much of the activity has completed or whether any problems have been encountered. If this is the case for your application, consider changing the glyph or the text in the icon to show the progress and completion of the activity.

You can also use the icon to alert users to problems encountered during the activity. For example, a compiler application typically takes a while to run. You could include a small graphic image that looks like a gauge in the icon that is filled or emptied as the compiling activity progresses. If an error is encountered, the icon could modify the image—such as showing the gauge broken in half. Other than showing that there is a problem, and perhaps indicating its severity, it is not important to provide more details in the icon image, because users will investigate the problem further in the opened window.

a) Is the application used only interactively?

b) Does the application run background tasks?

c) Does the icon need to inform users of a few essential conditions? If so, how can these conditions be represented?

Base Windows

Users often interact with applications by looking at information in a window and entering new information there. When an application is running, it is represented either by its icon (described in the previous section) or by a base window. The base window is the focal point of the application.

1 How do users interact with the application?

A clock is an application that usually does not require user input. A clock could be displayed as an icon. Opening the icon to a base window could provide time from other zones, the date, a fancier display, alarm settings, status, and so on. The icon itself is usually adequate for providing the information (the time) from the clock application.

A mail application, on the other hand, requires a great deal of user interaction that should take place in a base window. An icon for a mail application can show whether new mail messages are present, but cannot list the messages received nor contain information about each message.

2 What is the proper default size for a base window?

When they are opened, base windows have a default size that users can change. The window should be large enough to display the minimum amount of data users want to see when they start the application. For example, when using a desktop publishing package, users probably want to see an entire page in the base window, and will become annoyed if they keep having to resize the window to make it larger.

a) What is the minimum amount of information users want to see?

Make your best guess at the most reasonably convenient and useful minimum size for the window.

3 What is the largest reasonable size for a base window?

Although the base window should be large enough to show its vital information, as mentioned above, it should not totally obstruct the windows of other applications.

If the application is designed to be used on its own, and if it is likely that users will not be operating other applications simultaneously, the size consideration is less important. For example, users are less concerned with using a window that is the size of a piece of paper when they are sending short, plain text mail messages. When users are running an application on a dedicated system, they are less likely to be running other applications. The size of the monitor might also be a factor. Some systems have smaller, less sophisticated screens.

a) Will this application be used while other applications are running?

b) Will this application be running on a dedicated system?

c) Is the application likely to be run on systems with small screens?

4 Should the window be divided into multiple panes and, if so, how many should there be?

It is not a good idea to divide the window needlessly into more than one pane, nor is it a good idea to have too many panes. However, there are times when dividing the window into multiple panes is a good idea.

Consider dividing the window into multiple panes when multiple categories of information will be displayed simultaneously. The primary concern in designing applications with multiple panes is how to focus the attention of users. In some contexts, multiple panes can be distracting. If users naturally think of the information as divided, then additional panes make sense. For example, in a mail application, it makes sense to have one pane to display the message list and another pane to display individual messages. On the other hand, each type of message (new, unread, read, and so forth) should not have its own pane.

a) How many categories of information need to be displayed simultaneously?

b) What information needs to be displayed in various formats and what alternate views can users switch between?

If users might look at data with different perspectives, additional panes and windows might not be necessary. Consider displaying multiple views of the data inside an existing pane when users do not need to see both representations simultaneously. For example, in a file manager application, users might want to see data files displayed as icons. Alternatively, users might want to see files displayed as a text list. It is unlikely that users need to see both views at the same time. Therefore, a single pane can be used to switch between the views.

5 What are the major actions available to users? Are they based on how the information is displayed in the pane or on which pane contains the information?

Another way to decide on the number of panes is to look at the number of major activities available to users. For example, in a mail application the following actions could be tied to one of two panes:

Pane 1 contains a list of mail messages. Actions that can be taken include retrieving new mail messages, scanning the list of messages, deleting messages, and choosing messages to be read.

Pane 2 displays message text. Actions that can be taken include reading messages, composing new messages, responding to messages, and forwarding messages.

Actions common to both panes include copying, moving, and deleting message headers and message text.

a) What are the primary actions users will take in each pane?

b) Are there common actions for both/all panes?

6 Can pop-up windows be used to show additional information?

A single base window (which is standard) is adequate when there is a limited number of panes and/or when it is efficient for users to switch between multiple views. Sometimes users want simultaneous views.

Pop-up windows are subordinate windows. They are visually independent of base windows but cannot be displayed when the base window is closed. Here are some pros and cons for using pop-up windows:

☐ Pop-up windows are useful for displaying information in a set format, including settings and additional details.

☐ Using pop-up windows implies a hierarchy (this window is subordinate to the base window).

☐ Pop-up windows are not good for providing full functionality (or simulating the full functionality) of a base window.

☐ Pop-up windows cannot be closed to an icon, so information can be seen only when the window is displayed.

a) Which functions in your application lend themselves to being displayed in pop-up windows?

b) Is there a performance reason for using pop-up windows?

Pop-up windows are appropriate for actions that take a relatively short time to execute.

7 Should separate base windows be used?

An application can have more than one base window. Each base window is unaffected by the opening and closing of the other base windows. Generally, separate base windows are useful when the application runs distinct, simultaneous activities that offer users detailed information and/or explicit control. For example, a database application might use a separate base window for an update activity. The window would provide details of the activity and allow users to affect the operation. Because each base window has an associated icon, users can close the window while it runs its activity, look at the icon to check on general status information, and open the window as needed.

The database example represents a background operation initiated by users. Some applications, such as a mail application, always have background processes running. While users prepare mail messages in one window, another window serves as the in-box, displaying new mail when it arrives. Most of the time, users leave the in-box window closed, opening it only when the icon image changes to show that new mail has arrived and been incorporated into the mail application.

Separate base windows are useful when users perceive the operations represented by each window as independent activities. It should make sense for one base window to be open even if another one is closed. Users may be confused by a single activity that is divided into separate base windows.

Another deciding factor is whether each base window can make use of the functionality that is normally found in the base window control area. If a window does not require this functionality, the distinction between base and pop-up windows may become blurred.

Here are some advantages and disadvantages of using multiple base windows:

☐ Separate base windows are useful for providing full window function-ality for the additional window, such as saving, printing, editing, viewing, and changing properties.

☐ Each window accurately causes users to think of it as representing a totally independent function. As a consequence, it makes sense to users when the other base window(s) is closed.

☐ Each base window can be closed to an icon that can display essential status and that can be opened when necessary.

☐ Users may be confused by a single activity that is divided into separate base windows.

a) Which functions in your application lend themselves to being displayed in additional base windows?

b) Which functions have background processes, initiated by users, that take a long time to execute?

c) Which functions are always running when the application is active?

Control Area Menu Buttons

The control area of a window is the place in which your application displays frequently used controls. Once the application has been divided into the proper number of base windows and panes, users must be able to locate various commands and settings easily. A major advantage to a common operating environment like the OPEN LOOK UI is that any application that has been used before has already taught your users the basic operations. When you follow recommended conventions, you lessen your burden for teaching common operations to your users. Users need to learn only the unique aspects of your application.

Because most applications have functions related to filing, viewing data, editing, and setting properties, the OPEN LOOK UI recommends a standard set of menu buttons: File, View, Edit, Properties and, if needed, (application-specific) actions.

☐ Anything that affects the entire application (and that could implicitly affect objects that live in the application) is a File function. For example, creating, saving, printing, importing to, and exporting from a database query are all File functions.

☐ Anything that affects the perspective and details of the application and the application objects (so long as it does not permanently affect an object's recorded attributes) is a View function. For example, providing details about the query display or style of query display is a View function.

☐ Anything that affects the existence or state of objects that users can select is an Edit function. For example, deleting, copying, and inserting (existing or previously existing) database elements, such as tables, are Edit functions.

☐ Anything that changes an object's attributes is a Property function. For example, altering the attribute of the database element, such as tables, is a Property function. Such attributes include the short name of the table, the fully qualified name, write attributes, and keys.

☐ Anything that creates an object from scratch (not by replicating an existing object and not by changing the entire file—which is a File function) is an application-specific action. If there are several objects, they could be grouped together on a button menu. For example, a drawing application might have a menu button titled "Draw." The Draw menu might contain items for drawing objects such as circles, rectangles, and polygons.

☐ Anything that initiates an activity that is separate from filing, viewing, editing, and properties can be represented in the control area either as separate controls or as items on button menus. For example, a database application might have menu buttons titled "Update" and "Query" under which items for updating and querying the data base are located.

1 What functions relate to the input/output of the overall file?

Place all related commands and settings in the File menu. Which of the following standard commands apply to your application?

☐ **Load** opens a command window allowing users to view a list of file names. Users choose a file to load from the list or type in a file name.

☐ **Save** opens a command window allowing users to save the current file. The name of the current file is displayed automatically. Users can save the file using the old name, or they can type in a new file name.

☐   **Browse** is an optional command that activates a file manager or database that lists files. File managers and databases typically provide additional functionality for locating and manipulating files, therefore saving application builders from duplicating functionality. The basic loading and saving functions for the application should always be provided by the Load/Save function.

☐   **New** creates a new file.

☐   **Print** prints a selected portion or all of the file.

Do the following optional commands apply to your application?

☐   **Import** loads all or a selected portion of an object/file from another application into the existing object/file.

☐   **Export** saves all or a selected portion of the existing object/file to another object file in another application.

Import and Export allow data to be exchanged without requiring users to open another window or start another application. Import and export functions often include translation algorithms along with the ability to read various file types. A text editor, for example, might allow a user to import graphics from a drawing application. If the text editor understands the file format of the drawing application, the file can be read directly by the text editor without starting the drawing application.

Are there additional commands or settings you should put in the File menu?

☐   _____

☐   _____

2 What functions relate to the display of information in the base window?

A spreadsheet application, for example, could let users toggle between a numeric/columnar format and a plot/graph format. It could also allow users to switch between seeing cell values (data) or the cell formulae.

Place all commands and settings related to what information is displayed and how it is displayed in the View menu. Which of the following standard commands apply to your application?

☐   Display of magnification window (as in a drawing application)

☐   Display of grid points and rulers (as in a graphics application)

☐   Display of control characters (as in a communication application)

☐   Display of page guides (as in a desktop publishing application)

☐   Sort order (as in applications that list items)

☐   Display of alternate views (as in tabular versus graphical views for a spreadsheet application)

☐   Display of glyphs versus lists (as in file manager applications)

☐   Display of abbreviated or verbose descriptions and details (for objects displayed in the base window)

☐   Display of pop-up windows that provide additional details

Are there additional commands or settings you should put in the View menu?

☐   _____

☐   _____

3 What functions relate to the editing of information in the base window?

Place all commands and settings related to editing in the Edit menu. Which of the following standard commands apply to your application?

☐   **Select All** highlights all of the objects within a specific area.

☐   **Undo** reverses the previous action.

☐   **Again** repeats the previous action.

☐   **Cut** removes an object and places it on the clipboard (an edit buffer).

☐   **Copy** places an exact duplicate of the object on the clipboard.

☐   **Paste** inserts the contents of the clipboard at a selected location.

☐   **Delete** removes a selected object without affecting the clipboard.

☐   **Clear** clears the input area without requiring a selection.

Are there additional commands or settings you should put in the Edit menu?

☐   _____

☐   _____

4   **What functions relate to the settings and attributes of objects in the base window?**

Place all commands and settings related to setting attributes of objects in the Properties menu. Which of the following standard commands apply to your application?

☐   **Selection** provides settings for the highlighted object.

☐   **General** provides overall tool settings and user preferences.

Some objects are not easily selected by users. For example, designating a character, word, sentence, or paragraph is easy for users of a text-editing application to understand. Selecting an entire page, section, or chapter might not be so obvious. If your application has objects that cannot be selected, and if those objects have properties, list them.

Are there additional selections you should put in the Properties menu for objects that are not selectable or not intuitively selectable?

☐ _____

☐ _____

5 **What functions do not fall into the File, View, Edit, and Properties menu categories?**

Applications often include specific actions that execute functions or perform operations that do not fall into the previous four menu categories.

☐ When there are only a few of these functions or operations, and they are used frequently, each can be present in the control area.

☐ When there are several commands, group them in an appropriately labeled menu button. For example, "Create" would contain objects that users can create.

a) Which functions are so important or so frequently used that putting them inside the standard menus would be inconvenient for users? For example, in a mail application, users might feel that Previous and Next buttons for viewing mail messages are used so frequently that they should be displayed directly in the control area.

☐ _____

☐ _____

It is tempting to put frequently used functions directly in the control area. Do this only if every user will use these functions every time they use the application. Consider these possibilities for making frequently used controls available:

☐ Put frequently used controls in a menu that has a pushpin so that it can be permanently displayed at users' discretion.

☐ Put frequently used controls in command windows for additional flexibility.

An additional flexibility provided by the previous two options is that users can position the pinned menu at any location.

☐ Put frequently used controls in a pop-up menu that appears at the pointer location.

b) What small number of commands can be located directly in either the control area or in the application-specific menu?

☐ _____

☐ _____

c) What functions are so important that they should be displayed directly as command buttons in the control area?

☐ _____

☐ _____

d) Which functions can be grouped together as items on a button menu that should be located in the control area?

☐ _____

☐ _____

Objects and Properties

An object is any item that users can select and to which they can usually apply properties. For example, in a text-editing application, an object is selected text, which might be a character, a word, a sentence, or the entire document. In an object-oriented drawing application, an object can be a single, selectable graphic picture or a group of such pictures. In a raster-based application, an object might be a drawing canvas or a region of that canvas.

The effective and consistent use of property windows can help to make your application easy and intuitive to use. The information in this section addresses properties that users can set for objects that are a part of your application.

1   Which objects in your application can be selected?

2   Is there a familiar metaphor for each of the objects?

   Real-world metaphors make an application easier to use. For example, in a disk-formatting application, a glyph for a hard disk should look different from a glyph for a floppy disk, and each should bear some resemblance to the real-world object it represents.

3   Is there a graphical representation for the objects in your application that can be selected?

   As previously mentioned, it is ideal when your application contains objects that users recognize from real-world counterparts.

4   Which objects have properties?

   Users should be able to expect to find properties for every object. At any time that users select an object and press the Properties key on the keyboard or choose a Properties item, a property window should be displayed. For example, glyphs representing files would have properties such as the name, owner, access permissions, and file size. Properties for graphics objects include all variations of the aesthetic properties of the object. Text properties include information about the font, attribute/ emphasis, and size of a character.

Each object should have a property window. In most cases, the property window allows users to change various parameters about the object. Property windows also allow users to make multiple changes to an object, then apply all of the changes at one time. Using a property window to change attributes is much faster than using a menu, because each menu command is invoked immediately (and users have to wait between each invocation).

When you provide property windows for your application, menus get smaller, because you can place items that might otherwise go on menus inside property windows.

When there is no selection, your application should assume that users have selected the pane or the application itself. Choosing Properties should yield general application or pane settings that users can view and/or change. Application properties include those application properties supported by your OPEN LOOK toolkit, such as scaling size and background color.

5 What are the properties for the objects?

Each object should have an associated property window that displays more detailed information about the object. In most cases, users can change the settings in the property window to change the state of the selected object, but that is not required. Property windows can also be used to allow users to see information that they could not otherwise determine, even if they cannot change that information. For example, displaying a property window could reveal that a type font is 9 point without allowing users to change the point size.

List all of the attributes that can be changed by users, along with relevant read-only information.

6 Are there properties that apply to multiple object types?

Only related objects should be simultaneously selectable. Related objects are those that share one or more attributes that users might want to change simultaneously for all objects.

☐ When all of the properties of all the object types are the same, use a single property window.

☐ When some of the properties are different, a single property window can still be used, with inapplicable settings ignored for objects to which they do not apply. For example, if users select a rectangle and a circle in a graphics application and display a property window, they might be able to change properties such as the border color, width, style, and the interior color and pattern for both objects. If users selected a rectangle, a circle, and a line, and displayed the same property window, the border settings would apply to all of the objects, but the interior settings would apply only to the circle and the rectangle.

☐ Another possibility is to open a property window and provide one category for those settings that can be applied uniquely to the selected object and another category for those general properties that affect all selected objects.

a) Which objects in your application share similar properties?

b) Which ones have unique properties?

Command Windows

Command windows provide you with a place to group related commands, keeping them available so that they can be displayed and used at an appropriate time. Users can pin frequently used command windows and position them wherever they like on the workspace.

1 What actions can be taken with which objects?

All application functions that are not property attributes of the various objects are actions. For example, in a mail application, users can copy, move, delete, print, send, forward, read, and save mail messages, to name just a few of the actions. These are not attributes for an object but actions on an object.

a) To determine what actions operate on what objects in your application, create a matrix, listing all actions in a single column and all objects in a row across the top. Use check marks to indicate which actions apply to which objects.

b) Which actions are complex?

Some actions can be invoked directly. Other actions require additional information from users before they can be performed.

Put actions that require no arguments as items in menus. For example, deleting an object usually requires no arguments. Users select the object(s) and choose Delete.

Put actions that require additional information from users in a command window. For example, saving an object requires that users enter the name and directory where the object will be saved. It might also allow users to specify other information such as file format.

Put actions that might or might not require additional arguments but that are frequently taken along with other actions in a command window. For example, in a database application, users frequently might delete rows, update the database, then sort the rows again. Suppose each of these commands required no arguments from users. Also suppose that each of these commands took a few seconds and then caused the screen to refresh. If each was invoked from a menu, users would be forced to wait between each execution. If the commands were available in a command window, users could choose all three actions and press a single button. In addition, the command window could be pinned, keeping it on the screen and saving pointer travel to display a menu.

c) Using your matrix of commands and objects, circle each check mark that represents a command requiring arguments.

d) Create a separate list of command windows and note which commands can share command windows.

2 Which commands take a long time to execute?

Many commands are executed within a few seconds. When an operation takes longer, you might want to allow other actions to be performed during the command's execution. When a command is executed from a menu, the menu button displays the busy pattern until the command is complete. No other actions are allowed.

☐ Simple commands, such as editing operations, can be executed directly from menus. The message area of the window in which the command takes effect (usually the base window) should indicate the status of the command if the result is not evident to users. For example, if users delete an item from the screen, the fact that it is removed is enough feedback. However, if users delete one or more items that were not all visible, a completion message should inform users that x number of objects were deleted.

If a command takes a long time to execute, and it is initiated from a menu in the base window, consider displaying a status command window. The window could report the progress of the operation in a scrolling list, as a graph, as a gauge, as a percentage done, as numbers, as other symbols, or as a clock. Because users could close the pop-up window before the command is complete, display a message in the footer of the base window informing users of the number of background processes in progress. You could interactively add the name of the status window to the View menu so that users could redisplay the window if desired to check on the status of the activity. For example, if users begin a lengthy activity, such as updating a database, the update command could be invoked directly from a menu. A separate status command window could then be displayed to report on the progress and to allow users to cancel the update if they wish.

When an operation is very complex and lengthy, consider using a separate base window, as long as the separate base window makes sense when it stands alone. Users can then start an activity, close the window to an icon, and continue with other operations. The icon can display status as the activity continues, and users can open the base window to monitor the progress or affect the operation. For example, if a compiling application provides a separate base window for the compiling function, users could start compiling in a separate base window. Users would have the option of interacting with the activity or closing the window to an icon. The icon could flash and report status as required.

☐ More complex commands should be executed from command windows that stay open until the command is complete.

Command windows that initiate lengthy operations should have a button that permits a graceful interruption of the activity. For example, if users are saving a file, a command window is used to enter file information. During the actual saving, the window should remain displayed and in the footer a message should report on the progress (for example, "Waiting for file server to respond.")

a) On your matrix of commands, note those with lengthy execution times.

b) On the matrix, consider the window's "in progress" look. For example, add a Stop button if the activity can be interrupted.

c) If the operation is invoked directly from the menu and takes a while to execute, note the need for a status command window.

d) List operations that are complex and that require their own base windows.

A Final Note

This chapter has presented some of the general issues for you to consider in designing an application using the OPEN LOOK UI. It is impossible to devise a formula that can be used for designing all applications. The most important thing for you to keep in mind is that your application should stay in harmony with users' conceptual model. The guidelines provided in the rest of this book address more specific design issues.

3

An Overview of the OPEN LOOK Graphical User Interface

Designing the interface for a computer program can be compared to designing a house. Just as an architect works with a standard set of building blocks when designing a house, you work with a standard set of OPEN LOOK Graphical User Interface elements to design the way users communicate with your application. As an application developer, your task does not involve deciding which components are part of the interface itself. That work has already been done for you by the designers of the OPEN LOOK UI. Rather, your task is to decide which of the existing components to use in your application and how best to present them so that users of your application know almost immediately how to operate them.

An architect designing a house provides at least one door for each room. Similarly, when designing an OPEN LOOK UI application, you must provide certain elements of the OPEN LOOK UI to maintain consistency with the overall environment. It is important for you to know what users expect of an OPEN LOOK UI and what parts of the environment users can customize before you begin designing your application. Understanding the environment in which your application is presented and using the components—the controls and the required and optional window elements—of the OPEN LOOK UI ensures that your application is consistent with other OPEN LOOK UI applications.

This chapter provides a review of the workspace and application environments to help you understand the framework of your environment. If you are already familiar with the fundamentals of the OPEN LOOK UI, you can skip to Chapter 4, which begins the presentation of guidelines for developing applications for the OPEN LOOK UI. If you are not familiar with the fundamentals of the OPEN LOOK UI, refer also to the *OPEN LOOK Graphical User Interface Functional Specification.*

The Workspace

The overall structure in which applications are presented in an OPEN LOOK UI multitasking window environment is called the *workspace.* The workspace has a 50 percent gray pattern. In color implementations, it may have a lightly saturated color. On the workspace, an application is displayed in a small visual form as an *icon,* or as a larger rectangular or square work area called a *base window.* Each application typically also has a number of smaller, subordinate pop-up windows that users display, use, and dismiss at will. Within OPEN LOOK UI windows, you provide controls and menus that users activate to interact with the data of your application. Figure 3-1 shows a typical workspace with windows and icons.

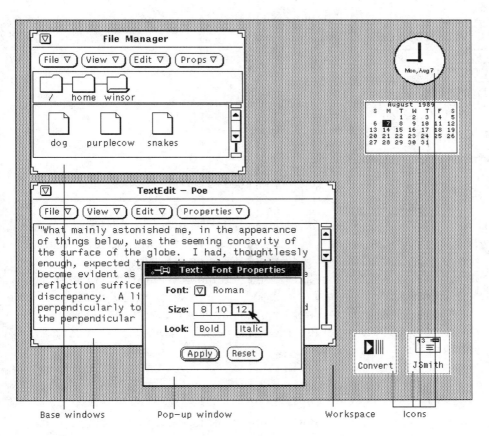

Figure 3-1   A typical workspace.

Workspace Menu

The workspace has its own menu, from which users can start up applications, access utilities, display the Workspace Properties window, or exit the OPEN LOOK UI environment. Figure 3-2 shows the default *Workspace menu*.

Figure 3-2   The default Workspace menu.

The Properties item on the Workspace menu displays the *Workspace Properties window*, from which users can customize the workspace environment. These properties apply to the system as a whole. When designing your application, consider that the settings that users modify from the Workspace Properties window have a direct effect on how your application works.

In a Level 1 implementation, users can customize the entries on the Programs submenu. In a Level 2 implementation, users can customize the Workspace menu and its submenus.

The Pointer

One of the smallest but most important elements on the workspace is the *pointer*. When users move the mouse or other pointer control device, the pointer moves on the workspace. The OPEN LOOK UI supports a variety of devices designed to move and position the pointer.

Because the *mouse* is the most common pointing device, this book refers to the mouse as the specific pointing device. Users manipulate objects by positioning the pointer on an object and pressing buttons on the mouse.

When users press a mouse button on an OPEN LOOK UI control, standard visual feedback shows that an action has been initiated or a choice has been made. If users do not want to complete the action, moving the pointer off the object and releasing the mouse button clears the feedback and does not complete the action.

The OPEN LOOK toolkit provides standard pointers for the following functions:

☐ Basic operation

☐ Move and duplicate operations

☐ Busy feedback

☐ An invalid action

☐ Text move and duplicate operations

☐ Scrolling the contents of a pane by panning

☐ Selecting a small target such as the border of the pane

Figure 3-3 shows the OPEN LOOK UI standard pointer shapes.

Basic pointer

Move pointer

Duplicate pointer

Busy pointer

Question mark pointer

Text move pointer

Text duplicate pointer

Panning pointer

Target pointer

Figure 3-3   Standard pointer shapes.

Your application can define additional pointer shapes for specialized functions. For example, a drawing application can display crosshairs when users choose a drawing operation. In addition to showing the function, crosshairs add to the precision with which the pointer is manipulated.

When the Pointer Changes Shape

In general, the pointer changes shape on the downstroke of a mouse button or its equivalent and returns to its previous appearance on the upstroke, when the button is released.

The busy pointer is the only pointer that is controlled by application behavior and not by user manipulation of a mouse button. The application determines when an action that must block input to a control or a window is being performed. When the action is complete, the application restores the pointer to its previous appearance, which is usually the basic pointer.

The OPEN LOOK UI specifies a small distance called the damping factor that allows users to make slight movements of the pointer without inadvertently moving an object. The toolkit sets the damping factor, which is usually 5 pixels. A *pixel* is an abbreviation for *picture element,* the smallest unit that can be displayed on a computer screen. When users initiate dragging operations, the pointer does not change shape until it is dragged beyond the damping factor.

The Mouse

Because the mouse is the most common pointing device, the OPEN LOOK UI specifies conventions for mouse functionality. It does not specify conventions for other pointing devices, although parallel functions should be supported.

Mouse Button Use

In the interest of consistency, the OPEN LOOK UI specifies strict conventions for how you use the mouse buttons. Three standard functions are defined, one for each button of a three-button mouse:

☐ *SELECT* includes the two most fundamental functions: specifying an object to operate on and manipulating objects and controls.

☐ *ADJUST* extends or reduces the number of selected objects.

☐ *MENU* displays a menu that is associated with the pointer location or the selected object.

The OPEN LOOK UI can be used with a one-, two-, or three-button mouse or with an alternate pointing device. If the mouse does not have three dedicated buttons for SELECT, ADJUST, and MENU functions, users can access the functionality by using modifier keys, such as pressing Control and SELECT together to access MENU functionality.

On a three-button mouse, the default assignments of the buttons are, from left to right: SELECT, ADJUST, and MENU. On a two-button mouse, the left button is used for SELECT, the right button for MENU, and the modified SELECT button for ADJUST. On a one-button mouse, the unmodified button is SELECT, with modifier keys required for the ADJUST and MENU functions. Figure 3-4 shows the default mouse button assignments for a one-, two-, and three-button mouse.

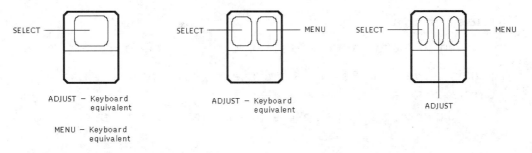

Figure 3-4   Default mouse button assignments.

Although applications should always use the default assignments, users can change them to accommodate personal preference, such as use by a left-handed person or for the sake of compatibility with other systems. For example, on a two-button mouse a user could assign ADJUST to the un-modified right mouse button and require a modifier key for MENU.

Mouse Terminology

This book uses the following terms to describe the actions users can take with the mouse and the pointer:

☐ *Press:* Push a mouse button and hold it.

☐ *Release:* Let up on a mouse button.

☐ *Click:* Push and release a mouse button before moving the pointer.

☐ *Double-click:* Push and release a mouse button twice in quick succession without moving the pointer.

☐ *Move:* Slide the pointer without pushing any mouse buttons.

☐ *Drag:* Push a mouse button and hold it down while moving the pointer.

The phrase "dragging an object" is short for "moving the pointer over an object, pushing the SELECT button on the mouse, moving the pointer until the object is in the desired new location, and releasing the SELECT button."

Mouse Settings

Users can set the following mouse and pointer characteristics:

☐ The ratio between the distance the mouse moves on the mouse pad and the distance the pointer moves on the screen

☐ The maximum time permitted between clicks (release and then press) for multiple clicking operations

☐ Whether or not the pointer moves automatically when certain actions are performed

Mouse Modifiers

The OPEN LOOK UI specifies keys that are used to modify mouse buttons. Users can customize the keys that modify mouse buttons for the following functions:

☐ *Duplicate* by dragging

☐ Scroll by *panning* (dragging the contents of a pane directly)

☐ *Constrain* the direction of a direct move or copy operation

☐ Set the *menu default*. Each OPEN LOOK UI menu must have a default item. Because users can change the menu default at any time, application functionality should never depend on a specific menu default item.

☐ Select a character

The Keyboard

The keyboard is the primary means of entering data. Although keyboards vary greatly in number and arrangement of keys, most keyboards include the following:

☐ The standard alphanumeric keys

☐ Modifier keys such as Shift and Control

☐ System function keys such as Home, End, Scroll up, Scroll down, and Delete

☐ Application function keys (typically F1 through F10)

☐ Miscellaneous keys such as arrows and those on the numeric keypad

Keyboard Core Functions

The OPEN LOOK UI permits users to store data in a temporary storage area called the *clipboard*. Users expect to be able to transfer data between applications by cutting or copying it to the clipboard in one application and pasting it into another application. The clipboard is used for the following three "core function" keys:

☐ *Cut* removes the selection from its present location and stores it on the clipboard.

☐ *Copy* puts a copy of the selection onto the clipboard.

☐ *Paste* inserts a copy of the information on the clipboard at a user-designated destination.

The following four core function keys are also required:

☐ *Help* displays a Help window containing information about the object area under the pointer.

☐ *Properties* displays settings for the selected object.

☐ *Undo* reverses the last operation.

☐ *Stop* stops the last action taking place at the pointer location.

Keyboard Miscellaneous Functions

The OPEN LOOK UI specifies a number of miscellaneous keyboard functions. The number of functions provided depends on the OPEN LOOK toolkit you are using. These keyboard functions permit users to perform commonly used operations without moving from the keyboard to the mouse. These operations include:

☐ Acting on pop-up windows from the keyboard

☐ Moving from one text field to another

☐ Moving the *insert point* (the place where characters are typed) forward or backward one character

☐ Deleting a character to the left or right of the insert point

Setting the Input Area

Users can choose one of two modes of operation to indicate the active area for keyboard input:

☐ Click-to-type in a window
☐ Move pointer into window

The default mode for the OPEN LOOK UI is click-to-type. In this mode, users move the pointer into the window and click the SELECT mouse button to designate the input area. Level 2 implementations provide an additional option that lets users set the input area on the workspace by simply moving the pointer into the window.

If you optimize your application design only for click-to-type mode, users who favor the move pointer option may find it difficult to use.

System Beeping

Users can choose which beeps generated by the system are audible. They can set the system so that it beeps whenever an application generates a beep, only when important messages are displayed, or never.

Window and Icon Characteristics

Users can set the following attributes for windows and icons:

☐ When this option is supported by your toolkit, users can change the size, or *scale*, of all window elements in relationship to one another.

☐ Some toolkits may provide an option that permits users to specify whether vertical scrollbars are positioned at the right or the left side of a pane. Horizontal scrollbars are always positioned below the pane.

☐ Users can choose the side of the screen (top, bottom, left, or right) that icons move to when an application is started or when a window is closed.

Users can also choose, in a color or grayscale implementation, whether or not an unselected icon is displayed with a border.

□ Some toolkits may allow users to define a *reserved area* of the workspace. Only icons and special application windows may be moved onto this reserved area.

The Workspace Grid

The workspace has a grid that determines how icons are positioned. Users can set the following properties for the workspace grid:

□ Whether icons automatically align with the invisible workspace grid

□ The point of origin for the workspace grid

□ The spacing for the workspace grid

Menu Properties

Users can customize certain properties that determine how they view and choose from menus. The properties that can be adjusted depend on the level and complexity of your toolkit.

Color

Color implementations permit users to set default colors for the workspace, for windows, and for the selection. Users can override the default window color, setting a different color for individual applications.

Controls

Just as the workspace provides an environment for your application, so the individual controls are part of the overall framework. Like the light switches in a room, some OPEN LOOK UI controls can be turned on and off. Other controls, like doorknobs, allow users to go into other parts of an application.

The way you combine the OPEN LOOK UI design elements is completely open and flexible, giving you a variety of ways to present choices and provide shortcuts for your users. However, using the controls and components of the OPEN LOOK UI maintains a consistent look and feel that users can depend on to behave in the same way regardless of what application they control. This section provides a brief review of the OPEN LOOK UI components.

Buttons

Buttons are used for single commands and are typically used in control areas. The name of the command is usually the title on the button. For example, to save a document, users would click SELECT on a button that says "Save." When a button has a *window mark*—three dots—following the label, choosing it causes a window to be displayed. The window can be either a base window (in applications with multiple base windows) or a pop-up window. Users then choose the command from the controls you provide in the window. Figure 3-5 shows a command button and a window button.

Figure 3-5   Examples of a command button and a window button.

Menu buttons are used to display menus containing additional controls. Menu buttons always have a *menu mark*, an outlined triangle following the label. The triangle points to where the menu is displayed. The menu for a menu button labeled "Insects" might have items labeled "Crickets," "Lady-bugs," and "Bumblebees."

When users press a button, it *highlights* to provide visual feedback.
Figure 3-6 shows an Insects menu button with the menu mark pointing down.
The Marsupials button has a menu mark pointing to the right. It is highlighted because its menu is displayed.

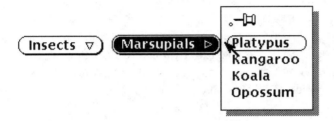

Figure 3-6   Examples of menu buttons and a button menu.

Menus

The OPEN LOOK UI provides three basic types of menus:

☐ *Button menus,* which users display by choosing a menu button
☐ *Pop-up menus,* which pop up at the pointer location and control the region under the pointer
☐ *Submenus*, which users display from other menus

Menus can have items and settings. Any menu, with its associated sub-menus, is called a *menu group.*

Figure 3-7 shows some examples of menus and menu groups.

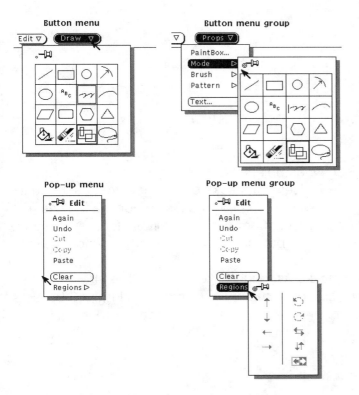

Figure 3-7 Examples of button and pop-up menus.

Items

Items are used to provide the same functionality as buttons. Just as command buttons, window buttons, and menu buttons are used in a control area, *command items*, *window items*, and *menu items* are used on menus. Items on menus have the same feel and functionality as buttons, but they have a slightly different look. Figure 3-8 shows examples of items.

Figure 3-8   Examples of items on a menu.

Exclusive Settings

Exclusive settings are used when objects selected by users have a state and that state can be changed. Users can make one choice from each group of settings. For example, each word in a word processing application has a font. Users can choose a different font from a list of available fonts that may be presented as exclusive settings, but they can choose only one font setting at a time.

Exclusive settings are displayed as touching rectangles. The chosen setting is shown with a bold border. In the example shown in Figure 3-9, users can run a spelling checker for only one language at a time, and French is the chosen setting.

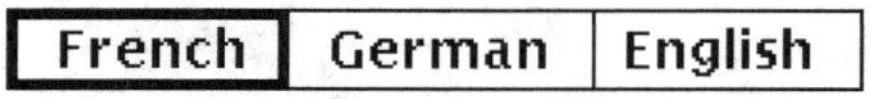

French	German	English

Figure 3-9   An exclusive setting.

When it is appropriate for your application, you can use a variation of exclusive settings that permits users to choose none of the settings.

Nonexclusive Settings

Nonexclusive settings are provided when users can set many values for one particular object. For example, text attributes such as bold, italic, and underline can all be set for the same word. Nonexclusive settings are displayed as separate rectangles. Users can choose all, none, or any combination of nonexclusive settings for the same object. In the example shown in Figure 3-10, an application showing aquarium inventory shows that an aquarium has displays for minnows, dolphins, and tuna, but not whales.

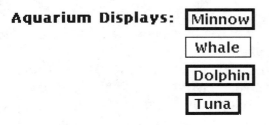

Figure 3-10   A nonexclusive setting.

Check Boxes

Check boxes are used to set a Yes/No or On/Off choice. Users can choose all, some, or none of the options by toggling the check box to display or suppress the check mark. In the example shown in Figure 3-11, socks are chosen, but shoes are not.

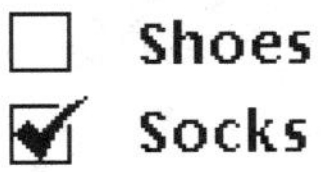

☐   **Shoes**
☑   **Socks**

Figure 3-11   Examples of check boxes.

Abbreviated Buttons

Abbreviated buttons provide the same functionality as buttons but take up less space. Abbreviated buttons are small square buttons with no text label inside them. They can have a glyph inside the button. Figure 3-12 shows abbreviated scrolling buttons.

Figure 3-12   Abbreviated scrolling buttons.

Abbreviated menu buttons are used when it is helpful to show the current choice without displaying a menu and when it is useful to save space. Abbreviated menu buttons are small square buttons with a menu mark inside the button. The label for the button is displayed to the left and the choice from the button menu is displayed to the right of the abbreviated menu button. Abbreviated menu buttons function the same way as menu buttons do. Figure 3-13 shows examples of an abbreviated menu button.

Marsupials: ▽ Platypus

Figure 3-13   An abbreviated menu button.

Text Fields, Text Regions, and Numeric Fields

Text fields allow users to type input from the keyboard. For example, a text field allows users to type the name of a document to save it. When a text field cannot display the entire text string, scrolling buttons are displayed to allow users to scroll the contents of the field. *Text regions* with borders and scrollbars permit multiline text entry. *Numeric fields* that can contain only numbers have increment/decrement scrolling buttons; users can click on them to increase or decrease the number displayed in the numeric field. Figure 3-14 shows some examples of text and numeric fields.

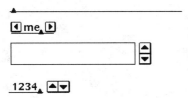

Figure 3-14 Examples of a text field, a text field with scrolling arrows, a text region with a minimum scrollbar, and a numeric field with increment/decrement buttons.

Sliders

Sliders are used to set a numeric value and give a visual indication of the setting. Sliders can have numeric fields and type-in fields. Sliders are used when an object has a range of possible settings. For example, sliders can be used to adjust the volume of a beep. Figure 3-15 shows a basic slider.

Figure 3-15 A basic slider.

Gauges and Read-Only Messages

Gauges are used to give a visual indication of how full or empty an object is or to show what percentage of a job is complete. Figure 3-16 shows an example of a gauge that shows disk usage.

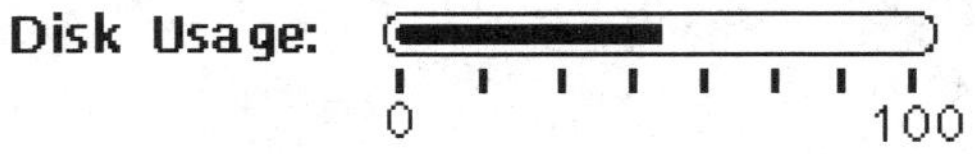

Disk Usage: ⊏█████████⊐
0   100

Figure 3-16   A gauge.

Read-only messages provide text and/or numeric information that users cannot edit. In the example shown in Figure 3-17, file size is shown in bytes.

Size: 1997 bytes

Figure 3-17   A read-only message.

Scrolling Lists

Scrolling lists are similar to settings. The basic purpose of a scrolling list is to present an unbounded list of items in a small, well-defined region. A scrolling list in its basic form is a list of items through which users can scroll. Scrolling lists are the most flexible type of OPEN LOOK UI control. The OPEN LOOK UI supports the following kinds of scrolling lists:

☐ A scrolling list from which users can choose one item (*exclusive scrolling list*). When a new item is chosen, that item automatically supersedes a previously chosen item.

☐ A scrolling list from which users can choose one or none of the items (*variation of exclusive scrolling list*)

☐ A scrolling list from which users can choose none, one, or multiple items (*nonexclusive scrolling list*). Users can choose as many or as few items from the list as they want.

Any of these scrolling lists can be *hierarchical*—they can permit users to access different levels of a structured data organization.

Each of these kinds of scrolling lists has a required Scrolling List menu, and users can edit the lists by choosing items from that menu. Cut/Copy/Paste functionality that uses the clipboard is also provided. Users choose an item in an exclusive or nonexclusive list in the same way they choose an exclusive or nonexclusive setting: by moving the pointer to an item and clicking the SELECT mouse button. A chosen item becomes *current* and displays a rectangle around it.

Exclusive Scrolling Lists

Exclusive scrolling lists have the following required elements, as shown in Figure 3-18:

☐ A vertical scrollbar
☐ A current setting for only one item at a time
☐ A Scrolling List menu with a Locate Choice item

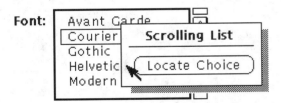

Figure 3-18 An exclusive scrolling list and its required menu.

The default menu for an exclusive scrolling list allows users to locate the current choice if it has been scrolled out of view. When the exclusive scrolling list can be edited, it also has an Edit List item to allow users to shift the list into edit mode.

Nonexclusive Scrolling Lists

Nonexclusive scrolling lists have the following required elements, as shown in Figure 3-19:

☐ A vertical scrollbar

☐ A current setting permitted for multiple items

☐ A Scrolling List menu with Locate Next Choice and Clear All Choices items

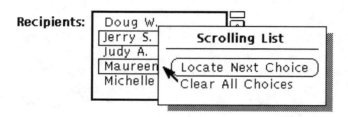

Figure 3-19 A nonexclusive scrolling list and its required menu.

The nonexclusive scrolling list menu provides users with an easy way to find the next item on the list that has been chosen. It also lets users clear all of the choices without scrolling through the list and turning them off individually. When the nonexclusive scrolling list can be edited, it also has an Edit List item to allow users to shift the list into edit mode.

Editing a Scrolling List

Your application can allow users to edit items in a scrolling list. For example, users might revise the name of an item, add a new one, delete an existing one, or change underlying data for an existing item. When a list can be edited, add the Edit List item to the bottom of the menu, as shown in Figure 3-20.

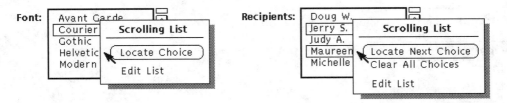

Figure 3-20 Default menus for a scrolling list with exclusive items (on the left) and a scrolling list with nonexclusive items (on the right).

When users choose Edit List, the scrolling list switches from displaying choices (represented by rectangles around the item) to showing selections (represented by highlighting the item). The rectangles around current items are dimmed. Users can then operate on the selected items in the scrolling list. In Figure 3-21, the "Jerry S." item is selected. Users select items using the SELECT mouse button.

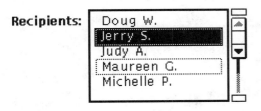

Figure 3-21 A scrolling list in edit mode with one item selected.

When users are editing the scrolling list, the default menu contains items for changing, inserting, or deleting selected items from the scrolling list and for ending the editing session. Figure 3-22 shows the minimum Scrolling List edit menu.

Figure 3-22 The minimum Scrolling List edit menu.

When an item on the scrolling list has associated information that is not displayed in the list, the first item in the default Scrolling List edit menu is not Change but Properties, as shown in Figure 3-23. Choosing the Properties item displays a property window containing all of the information for the selected item.

Figure 3-23 The minimum Scrolling List edit menu for a list with associated information.

When users have finished editing the scrolling list, they choose End Editing to return the scrolling list to its normal mode, from which users choose items for interaction with your application.

Hierarchical Scrolling Lists

Hierarchical scrolling lists give users a way to browse through a collection of items that has a natural hierarchical structure. Hierarchical scrolling lists have the following required elements:

☐ A title area

☐ Scrolling buttons at the right of the title area

☐ A Levels menu attached to the scrolling buttons. The application interactively updates the items on the Levels menu to reflect previously accessed levels of the hierarchy.

☐ Zero or more dots above the title that represent the place the level occupies in the hierarchy

☐ Glyphs or dots to the left of each item that has other items in the hierarchy within it

In the example shown in Figure 3-24, the hierarchy is a personnel directory for a company. Items in the list can represent either people or departments. The dots to the left of each item indicate that the item has additional items within it. The name of the item whose content is currently visible appears in bold at the top of the list. Above this title, the current level is "West Coast," and there is one level above West Coast in the hierarchy.

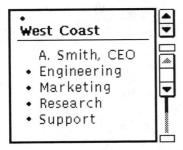

Figure 3-24 An example of a hierarchical scrolling list.

When users click SELECT on a list item that contains other items, is high-lighted but not opened. In some applications, users might want to designate a level in the hierarchy without indicating specific items within it. For example, a mail application might use a hierarchical scrolling list for designating mail recipients. If various departments are represented as levels in the hierarchy, users could choose an entire level without descending into it, thereby indicating that all department members are to receive the message.

Summary of Scrolling List Elements

Table 3-1 summarizes required and optional basic scrolling list elements.

Table 3-1   Summary of basic scrolling list elements.

Element	Usage	
	Required	Optional
Vertical scrollbar	☑	☐
Current setting	☑	☐
Scrolling List menu	☑	☐
Editing capability	☐	☑

Table 3-2 summarizes the required and optional hierarchical scrolling list elements.

Table 3-2   Summary of hierarchical scrolling list elements.

Element	Usage	
	Required	Optional
Vertical scrollbar	☑	☐
Current setting	☑	☐
Scrolling List menu	☑	☐
Editing capability	☐	☑
Title area	☑	☐
Title	☑	☐
Scrolling buttons	☑	☐
Levels menu	☑	☐
Hierarchy dots in title area	☑	☐
Hierarchy dots for items	☑	☐

Summary of Controls

To provide you with an overview of the OPEN LOOK UI controls, Figure 3-25 shows an example of each one.

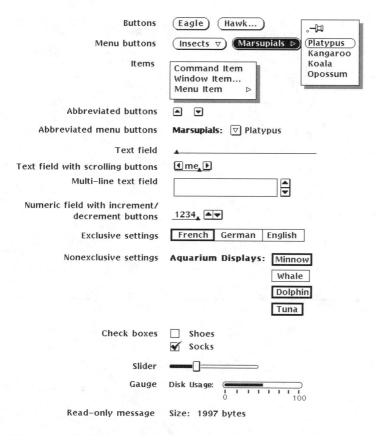

Figure 3-25 Examples of OPEN LOOK UI controls.

Table 3-3 summarizes the OPEN LOOK UI controls, and shows where they are used.

Table 3-3 Summary of controls and where they are used.

Control	Usage			
	Control Area	Menu	Pane	Header/ Footer
Abbreviated buttons	☑	☐	☑	☐
Abbreviated menu buttons	☑	☐	☑	☑ *
Check boxes	☑	☐	☑	☐
Command buttons	☑	☐	☑	☐
Command items	☐	☑	☐	☐
Exclusive settings	☑	☑	☑	☐
Gauges	☑	☐	☑	☐
Menu buttons (and their menus)	☑	☐	☑	☐
Menu items	☐	☑	☐	☐
Nonexclusive settings	☑	☑	☑	☐
Numeric fields	☑	☐	☑	☐
Pop-up menus	☐	☐	☑	☐
Read-only messages	☑	☐	☑	☑
Scrolling lists	☑	☐	☑	☐
Sliders	☑	☐	☑	☐
Text fields	☑	☐	☑	☐
Window buttons	☑	☐	☑	☐
Window items	☐	☑	☐	☐

* The Window menu button is an abbreviated menu button that is provided by the OPEN LOOK toolkit for the header of each base window.

Component Overview

The OPEN LOOK UI has a structure of elements that are common to the whole environment—the workspace, the ways users can customize it, and a simple set of controls. To build further on that foundation, the OPEN LOOK UI specifies the look and feel of certain components of the application environment, which include common elements of menus and base and pop-up windows.

Continuing with the architectural analogy, the application environment is like the doors, windows, and floor of the house. All of the rooms (applications) under the roof of this house share these elements. Not all rooms always have the same elements. Some rooms, for example, may have skylights. The OPEN LOOK UI also has optional elements that you can provide for each window. You may not necessarily provide these optional elements in your application, but when you do, the optional functionality should use the visual and functional design provided in the OPEN LOOK toolkit.

The rest of this chapter describes the look and feel for the following elements of the OPEN LOOK UI environment that provide the structural framework in which you present your application to users:

☐ Base windows

☐ Panes

☐ Pop-up windows

  ◻ Command windows
  ◻ Property windows
  ◻ Help windows
  ◻ Notices

Applications must work well with other applications to present a cohesive system. Users expect consistency on the workspace and they want control over their own environment. Well-behaved applications that consistently provide the common elements of the OPEN LOOK UI provide users with that benefit.

Base Windows

The base window is the primary window in which you present your application. When users are working in your application, the base window is where they look for controls, and the place from which they display menus and pop-up windows to operate on the data in the base window.

Standard base windows always have the following required elements:

☐ The standard base Window menu

☐ A header, with the title of the application and a Window menu button at the left

☐ An iconic representation

☐ At least one of the following two elements:

  ▫ A control area
  ▫ A pane

In addition to the required elements, the OPEN LOOK UI specifies a number of optional controls that you do not need to use for every window. When included, optional functionality should look and act in the way that is specified by the OPEN LOOK UI. For example, when you want to allow users to control the size and shape of the windows, the OPEN LOOK UI provides a control element called *resize corners* that look and act the same for each resizable window. When you want users to be able to resize a window, you add these resize corners to the window.

Standard base windows may have the following optional elements, if needed by your application:

☐ Resize corners

☐ A footer for displaying one-line status and error messages

☐ Long-term messages, such as the name of a file, can be displayed in the header following the application title

Figure 3-26 shows a typical base window.

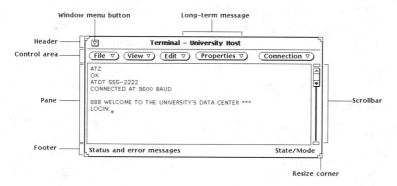

Figure 3-26   A typical base window with required and optional elements.

Base Window Menu

Each base window must have a base Window menu, shown in Figure 3-27, which users access by pressing MENU anywhere on the window background. The *window background* is any part of the window not covered by pane or a control. Panes, controls, and menus are in the *foreground*.

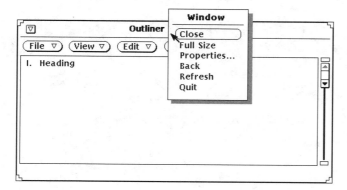

Figure 3-27   The required base Window menu.

The controls on the base Window menu allow users to perform the standard window management functions of closing the window to an icon, expanding it to full size, changing generic window properties, moving it to the back of the workspace behind any overlapping windows, repainting the entire window, and quitting the application.

Header

The base window must have a *header* with a Window menu button. Users click SELECT on the Window menu button to choose the default item from the base Window menu, or they use the MENU mouse button to display and choose from the Window menu.

You determine the title of the application and specify any long-term messages to be displayed in the header. See Chapters 7 and 9 for more information about application titles and long-term messages.

Footer

The base window usually has a *footer* that you can use to display status, error, and state or mode messages. See Chapter 9 for more information about messages.

Resize Corners

You determine which windows in your application can be resized. When a window can be resized, it has four resize corners with which users can change the area of the window. Typically, base windows have resize corners, and pop-up windows do not. You decide which windows in your application users should be able to resize.

Figure 3-28 shows how users can increase the area of a window by dragging the lower right resize corner.

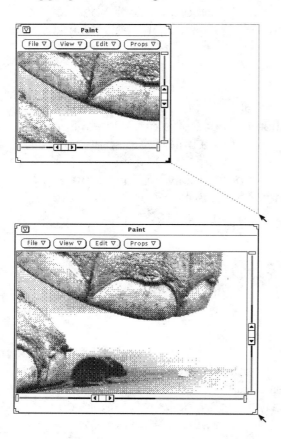

Figure 3-28   Resizing a window by dragging a resize corner.

Icon

Each base window must have its own unique icon. Icons typically contain both an image and a short text label, as shown in Figure 3-29.

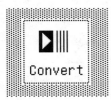

Figure 3-29 A typical icon.

Applications with multiple base windows may share the same application image and have a different label. Each icon has a base Window menu, with the first item labeled Open instead of Close.

Summary of Base Window Elements

Table 3-4 summarizes required and optional base window elements.

Table 3-4   Summary of base window elements.

Element	Usage	
	Required	Optional
Base Window menu	☑	☐
Header	☑	☐
Window menu button	☑	☐
Application title	☑	☐
Long-term message	☐	☑
Icon	☑	☐
Control area*	☐	☑
Pane*	☐	☑
Resize corners	☐	☑
Footer	☐	☑

* Each window must have at least one pane or control area.

Window Properties

Just as users can customize the workspace environment, so they can customize the environment for individual applications. The OPEN LOOK UI specifies a set of window properties that users access from the base Window menu Properties item. When you are designing your application, remember that users can override some of your default settings from this Property window.

The properties that users can customize are summarized below:

☐ The background color for application windows in color implementations

☐ The default area of the base window

☐ Where the window is displayed on the screen when the application is started

☐ Whether pop-up windows are open or closed when the application is started

☐ The default settings for each menu of the application environment

☐ Whether pop-up windows are grouped with the base window for certain operations

☐ The scale of base and pop-up windows

Figure 3-30 shows a complete set of window properties. This set of properties may vary from toolkit to toolkit.

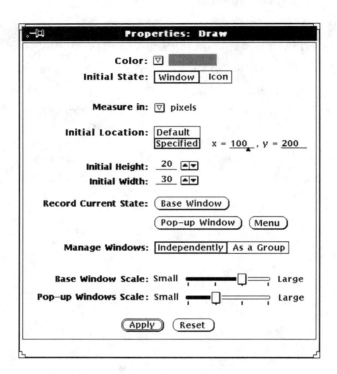

Figure 3-30   A complete set of window properties.

Scaling Windows. One Level 2 window property that bears special mention is the *Scale* property. Scaling makes everything in the window bigger or smaller while keeping all elements of the window proportional to one another. Scaling is useful to accommodate different tasks as well as differences in eyesight or ambient lighting conditions. For example, users might want to make a system message window smaller than normal or make a particular window larger than normal when giving a demonstration.

The scale control allows users to specify independently the scale of base windows and pop-up windows. Figure 3-31 shows a window in two scaling sizes.

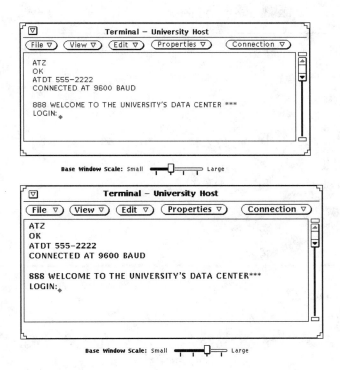

Figure 3-31 Window scaling.

Summary of Window Properties. Table 3-5 summarizes required window properties and shows which properties are required for a Level 1 and a Level 2 implementation. The color property is required only for color implementations, regardless of the level of implementation.

Table 3-5   Summary of required window properties.

Element	Usage		Provided By	
	Required	Optional	Level 1	Level 2
Color	☐	☑	☐	☑
Initial state	☑	☐	☑	☐
Units of measure	☑	☐	☐	☑
Initial location	☑	☐	☑	☐
Initial size	☑	☐	☑	☐
Record current base window state	☑	☐	☑	☐
Record current pop-up window state	☑	☐	☐	☑
Record current menu state	☑	☐	☐	☑
Group windows	☑	☐	☐	☑
Scale	☑	☐	☐	☑

Panes

Panes are the bordered areas in which you present your data to users. Users can typically display data in panes in various configurations, enter new data, delete old data, or edit existing data. You determine the number and location of panes within each window of your application. The OPEN LOOK UI specifies that each pane must always have an associated pop-up menu. You determine the name of the pop-up menu and the choices available on that menu. See Chapters 4 and 8 for more information about pop-up menus in panes.

Applications can provide the following optional functionality for panes. When you provide this functionality, it should work as specified by the OPEN LOOK UI.

☐ Scrolling

☐ Selectable pane border

☐ Resizable adjacent panes

☐ Splittable pane

☐ Joining of split panes

Scrolling

You determine the way users can scroll through the data in a pane. The OPEN LOOK UI supports two kinds of *scrolling*:

☐ *Panning:* Users can move the view of the data in the pane directly by dragging.

☐ Scrolling with a scrollbar: Users can move the view of the data by manipulating the OPEN LOOK UI scrollbar.

Scrollbars are a special type of control that make it easy for users to view objects—such as drawings, documents, and spreadsheets—that extend beyond the size of a pane. An OPEN LOOK UI scrollbar resembles an elevator riding on a cable suspended between two anchors. Figure 3-32 shows both a vertical scrollbar with its components labeled and a horizontal scrollbar.

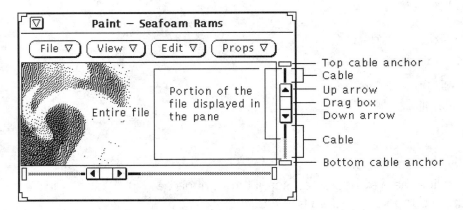

Figure 3-32 A pane with vertical and horizontal scrollbars.

Scrollbars are also displayed next to scrolling lists and, optionally, next to multiline text areas. The scrollbar conveys two interesting pieces of information at a glance. First, the location of the elevator on the cable corresponds to the location of the visible portion of the data in relation to the entire file. Second, the dark area of the scrollbar cable, the *proportion indicator*, gives users a rough idea of how much of the object is visible in the pane.

Scrollbar Proportion Indicator

The size of the proportion indicator is inversely proportional to the size of the object. The bigger the black part of the cable, the smaller the file. If the cable is all black, the entire file is visible. If the black part is just a small nub, the object is very large in relation to the pane. Figure 3-33 shows how to interpret the proportion indicator.

Figure 3-33   A scrollbar proportion indicator.

Scrollbar Usage

Users scroll through the data in the pane by manipulating the scrollbar with the mouse, as shown in Figure 3-34. Users can press the SELECT mouse button to repeat the action for those controls with an asterisk.

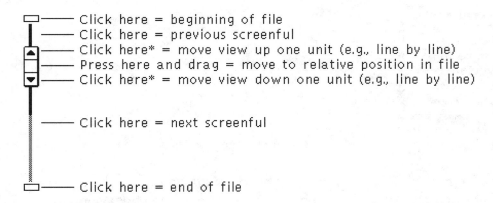

Figure 3-34   A functionally annotated scrollbar.

When a window is resized or a pane is split, the scrollbar grows and shrinks to accommodate the size of its pane, as shown in Figure 3-35.

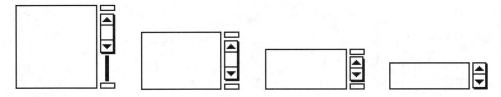

Figure 3-35 The scrollbar grows and shrinks to fit its pane.

Scrollbar Menu

Each scrollbar has its own Scrollbar menu, with a set of required items as shown in Figure 3-36.

Figure 3-36 The vertical Scrollbar menu for a pane that has been split.

Users can scroll a particular line to the top of the pane (or the reverse) and return to the previous scrolling location. When a pane can be divided to provide multiple views into the same data, or *split*, an item labeled Split View is added to the Scrollbar menu. Once a pane has been split, an item labeled Join Views is added to the Scrollbar menu.

You can add your own commands to expand the functionality of the Scrollbar menu.

Scrollbars with Page Orientation

For applications in which the data is naturally divided into pages, Level 2 OPEN LOOK toolkits provide *page-oriented scrollbars*. As users drag a page-oriented scrollbar, a box showing the current page number is displayed next to the scrollbar elevator, as shown in Figure 3-37.

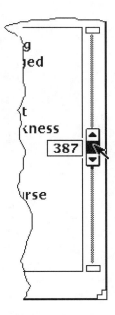

Figure 3-37   A page-oriented scrollbar.

The page-oriented scrollbar allows users to scroll directly to the desired page. When the mouse button is released, the elevator snaps into position so that the page begins at the top of the pane.

Selecting the Pane Border

A pane can be selected when it is useful to apply properties to all the data available in that pane, or when the pane can be resized. Users move the pointer onto the pane border. Because the border is thin, the target pointer is displayed when the hot spot is moved on the border of the pane. Users click SELECT, and the border of the pane thickens, as shown in Figure 3-38.

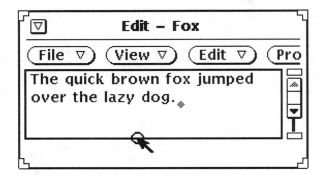

Figure 3-38 Selecting a pane.

Pane Resizing

When you allow users to adjust the area between two adjacent panes, the selected pane border displays *resize handles* on the sides of the pane that can be adjusted. Users can drag the resize handle to adjust the area between adjacent panes, as shown in Figure 3-39.

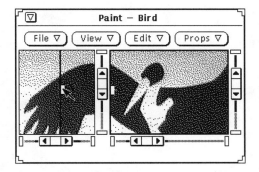

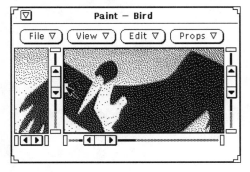

Figure 3-39   Resizing a pane by dragging a resize handle.

Pane Splitting and Joining

Panes that can be split have scrollbars, which are also used for splitting and joining panes. Users can split a pane either by dragging one of the cable anchors and releasing it to create multiple views into the same data, or by using the Split View item on the Scrollbar menu. Figure 3-40 shows how to split a pane using the cable anchors.

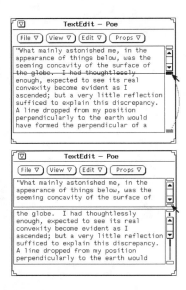

Figure 3-40 Splitting a pane by dragging a cable anchor.

Users join split panes either by dragging one of the cable anchors until it overlaps the other cable anchor for the pane and then releasing it, or by using the Join Views item on the Scrollbar menu. Figure 3-41 shows how to join views using the Scrollbar menu.

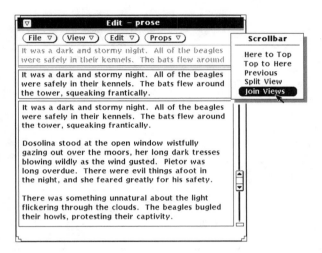

Figure 3-41   Joining views using the Scrollbar menu.

Summary of Pane Elements

Table 3-6 summarizes required and optional pane elements.

Table 3-6   Summary of pane elements.

Element	Usage	
	Required	Optional
Pane	☐	☑
Pop-up menu	☑	☐
Panning	☐	☑
Scrollbar	☐	☑
Scrollbar menu	☑	☐
Selectable border	☐	☑
Resize handles	☐	☑
Splittable panes	☐	☑

Pop-up Windows

In addition to the base window, the OPEN LOOK UI provides four kinds of *pop-up windows* that users can display and dismiss from the base window of the application:

☐ *Command windows* set parameters and execute commands based on those parameters.

☐ *Property windows* set more persistent properties associated with an object, an application, or a window.

☐ *Help windows* display help text for the area under the pointer.

☐ *Notices* are special pop-up windows that are used to display messages and conditions that must be brought to the user's attention.

All pop-up windows except Notices have the following required elements:

☐ The standard pop-up Window menu
☐ A header with the title of the application and a pushpin

All pop-up windows except Notices can have the following optional elements:

☐ A footer
☐ Resize corners

The Pop-up Window Menu

The *pop-up Window menu*, shown in Figure 3-42, lets users dismiss the pop-up window, move it to the back of the screen, redisplay or repaint it, or locate its owner.

Figure 3-42   The required pop-up Window menu.

The Pushpin

The pushpin on the left side of the header allows users to decide whether to use a pop-up window for quick, "one-shot" operations or whether to keep it on the screen for repeated operations. The pushpin has two states, as shown in Figure 3-43.

Figure 3-43 An unpinned and pinned pushpin.

When the pin is on its side, the window is in an unpinned state and is dismissed as soon as users click on a button to initiate an action. When users click on the pushpin, it pops into the hole beside it. Once the window is pinned, it remains displayed until users explicitly dismiss it by clicking on the pin a second time to pop it out of the hole, by choosing Dismiss from the Window menu, or by using the Cancel keyboard equivalent.

Command Windows

Command windows only have one additional required element: When a Command window has a button or buttons, one of them must be specified as the default, as shown in Figure 3-44.

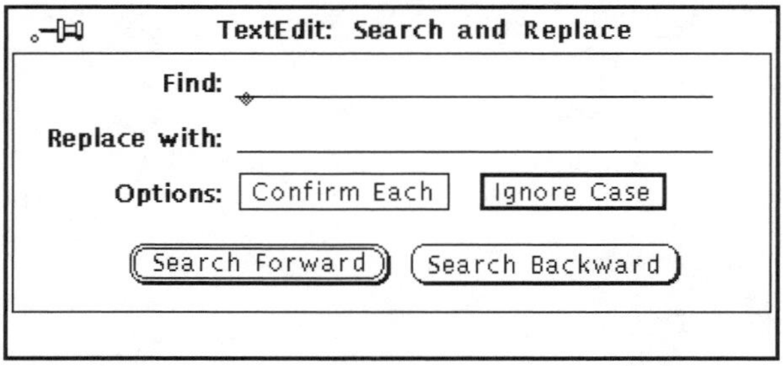

.–囗	TextEdit: Search and Replace
Find:	
Replace with:	
Options:	Confirm Each Ignore Case
	(Search Forward) (Search Backward)

Figure 3-44 A typical command window with a default button.

88

Property Windows

Property windows give users a way to view and modify the characteristics, or properties, of an object. Users first select the object of interest, and then display a property window.

All property windows have at least two buttons, as shown in Figure 3-45:

☐ *Apply:* Applies the changes users have made to the selected object and dismisses the property window if it is unpinned

☐ *Reset:* Discards any changes that users have made but have not yet applied, so that the controls in the property window reflect the current state of the object

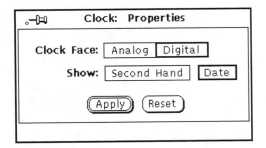

Figure 3-45 A typical property window with Apply and Reset buttons.

One optional button, *Set Defaults*, permits users to record new default settings for an individual property window.

OPEN LOOK UI property windows remember the original selection and one subsequent selection at the same time so that users can make other selections anywhere on the workspace without losing the original selection for the property window. When a property window for your application supports a second selection of the same kind within the same window, the Apply button is changed to an Apply menu button with the items Original Selection and

New Selection. This mechanism allows users to make a selection and easily apply the properties from that selection to other objects in the application.

Property windows also must have a Settings pop-up menu with items that match the functions provided at the bottom of the pane. The Settings menu shown in Figure 3-46 has all the required items.

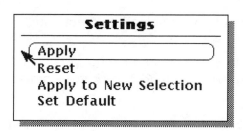

Figure 3-46 The property window Settings menu.

Help Windows

The OPEN LOOK toolkit provides the help text for the standard elements of base and pop-up windows and for the required menus. Applications must provide help text for each element of the application so that users perceive the Help window as consistently useful, whether the pointer is in an application or on one of the standard OPEN LOOK UI elements.

The Help window has the following required elements, as shown in Figure 3-47:

□ A *magnifying glass* at the left of the help pane that displays the object under the pointer

□ A pane that displays ten lines of help text for the object in the magnifying glass

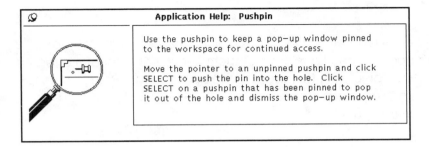

Figure 3-47 A Help window displaying information about the pushpin.

When the help message is longer than the standard ten-line Help pane, a scrollbar and resize corners are added automatically to the Help window, as shown in Figure 3-48.

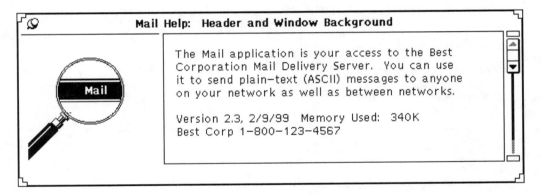

Figure 3-48 A Help window displaying information about an application.

Notices

A Notice is a special type of pop-up window used by the application to inform users of important conditions or to let them know that a serious error has occurred. Notices block all other input to the application, forcing users to respond before doing anything else. Notices have the following required elements, as shown in Figure 3-49:

☐ A default button

☐ When this feature is supported by the toolkit, Notices appear to pop out of the screen, with diverging lines projecting from the button that originated the notice. This tells users at a glance the origin of the Notice.

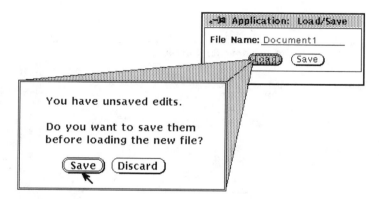

Figure 3-49   A Notice for confirming a Load operation.

See Chapter 9 for guidelines about using Notices.

Summary of Pop-up Window Elements

Table 3-7 summarizes required and optional pop-up window elements.

Table 3-7   Summary of pop-up window elements.

Element	Usage	
	Required	**Optional**
Header	☑	☐
Pushpin	☑	☐
Title	☑	☐
Pop-up Window menu	☑	☐
Command windows		
Default button	☑	☐
Property windows		
Apply and Reset buttons	☑	☐
Set Defaults button	☐	☑
Apply menu button	☐	☑
Settings pop-up menu	☑	☐
Help windows		
Magnifying glass	☑	☐
Notices		
Default button	☑	☐
Three-dimensional shadow	☐	☑

4

WINDOW CONFIGURATION

Introduction

Before you decide what controls to use and how to arrange them in your application, it is useful for you to divide application functions and controls into logical groupings. Now that you have basic information about the OPEN LOOK Graphical User Interface environment and controls, you can begin deciding how to fit your application into this framework. It is like deciding on the number of rooms and how they will be used when designing a house. If you do lots of entertaining, you probably want to include a formal dining room in your design. On the other hand, if you like the feeling of coziness and informality associated with eating in the kitchen, you want that room to be big enough to allow family members to congregate there without interfering with cooking activities. In the same way, determining which application operations are available directly and obviously in the base windows and which operations are available through a less direct route sets the tone and feel for your application.

The information in this chapter is designed to help you decide on the overall configuration and presentation of your application. It includes guidelines on the following topics:

☐ Base window design and configuration

☐ Pop-up window design and configuration for:
  ▫ Command windows
  ▫ Property windows
  ▫ Help windows
  ▫ Notices

☐ Menus/controls/pop-up window trade-offs

☐ Window characteristics, including how your application responds to resizing of windows and panes, types of scrolling in panes

Base Windows

The base window is the place where users interact with your application. A typical application has a single base window with a control area at the top containing a standard set of menu buttons. A pane for displaying and manipulating data is usually displayed immediately below the control area, as shown in Figure 4-1.

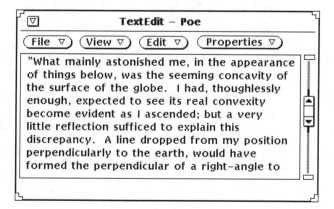

Figure 4-1   Standard base window layout.

Standard Menu Buttons

Four of the most common activities in an application are:

☐ Filing: Creating, saving, loading, and printing files
☐ Viewing: Controlling how data is displayed in the application
☐ Editing: Making changes to data
☐ Properties: Setting properties for data, usually for selected objects

Therefore, it is recommended that you provide File, View, Edit, and Properties menu buttons in that order, as shown in Figure 4-2, as standard controls in the control area. Use the menus attached to each menu button to present those standard functions to your users. This will ensure that your application is as consistent as possible with the other OPEN LOOK UI applications and that users can make valid assumptions about where to find certain standard functionality. See Chapter 6 for more information about the standard menu buttons.

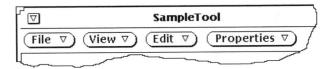

Figure 4-2   Standard control area with File, View, Edit, and Properties menu buttons.

☑ Put frequently used controls and features in the control area of your base window, where users can easily find them.

☑ If the functions your application provides do not fit neatly into the categories, by all means, use categories that make sense for your users.

☑ If you do choose to depart from the standard control area layout, make sure that you use a consistent layout across all of your applications.

Adding to the Standard Controls in the Control Area

You can put frequently used controls of any other type—buttons, settings, check boxes, text fields, sliders, and gauges—in your base window control area.

☑ Consider whether you should add other frequently used controls to the control area.

☑ If most of your users need to access a function directly most of the time, put that function on a button in the control area or in the pop-up menu for the pane so that it is easily accessible.

How Users Access Other Parts of Your Application

The following controls and menus that you provide in the base window of your application guide users to other, less obvious parts of your application:

☐ Window buttons provide access to other windows in your application.

☐ A menu button always has a menu or menu group attached to it.

☐ Pop-up menus contain frequently used commands and can also contain controls that access other parts of the application.

Menus can contain the following controls:

☐ *Command items* that take effect immediately

☐ *Window items* that display a window presenting additional choices and information to users

☐ *Menu items* that display a submenu containing additional choices

☐ *Settings*, either exclusive or nonexclusive, that affect the state of the selection

You can provide commands on the standard menus that perform the requested function directly. You can also provide commands that display pop-up windows that permit users to provide additional information to expand on the needed functionality. See Chapter 8 for more information about menus.

Diagramming Application Functionality

Creating a diagram for your application can help you visualize its organizational framework and prevent you from duplicating functionality or titles for pop-up windows. Figure 4-3 shows an expanded view of the suggested standard File menu (which is explained in detail in Chapter 6) as an example of one way to diagram the organization for your application.

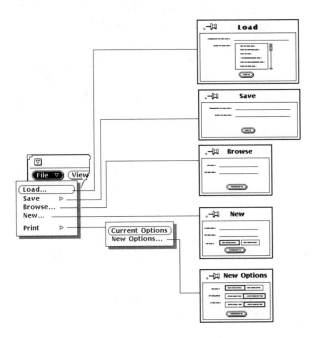

Figure 4-3   Expanded view of a standard File menu.

☑ Organize your application to create clear and logical paths for users to traverse to find the final command, minimizing a labyrinthine effect.

Alternate Base Window Layouts

The standard layout of a single control area and single pane works well for applications that deal with only one object. Typical examples include text editing, paint, draw, and spreadsheet applications that display only one file at a time.

Sometimes this simple structure is not enough. For example, when designing a mail application, you may want to allow users to browse through a list of messages and read and compose multiple messages. In a file manager, you may want to allow users to view both the directory tree and the contents of a given directory. This section offers guidelines for accommodating such situations by using the following:

☐ Multiple panes

☐ Multiple control areas

☐ Control areas in nonstandard locations

☐ Multiple base windows

Multiple Panes

You can use multiple panes with a single control area or with a control area for each pane.

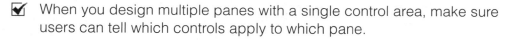 When you design multiple panes with a single control area, make sure users can tell which controls apply to which pane.

The mail application example shown in Figure 4-4 has a single control area and two panes.

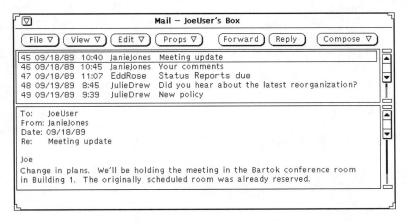

Figure 4-4   A good example of one control area and multiple panes.

The layout in this example works well, because the standard menu buttons on the left apply to both panes, and the Compose menu functions open other windows.

Figure 4-5 shows a good example of a window with multiple panes, each with its own control area. This layout works well because it is clear that the buttons in the top control area apply to the top pane and the buttons in the second control area apply to the bottom pane.

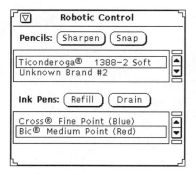

Figure 4-5 A good example of multiple panes, each with its own control area.

Figure 4-6 shows the same application with a confusing control area. It is not clear which controls apply to which pane.

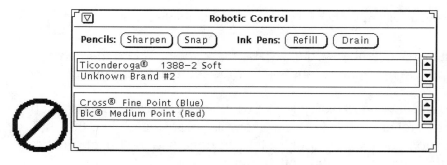

Figure 4-6 A bad example of one control area and multiple panes.

Alternate Control Area Layouts

Control areas are not restricted to the top of the window. Because users normally view information from left to right and top to bottom, it is natural for controls in a control area to read from left to right, and for a control area to contain controls that affect the data in the pane next to it.

☑ Position control areas in the base windows above or to the left of a pane.

Figure 4-7 shows a window with two control areas, one above and another to the left of the pane.

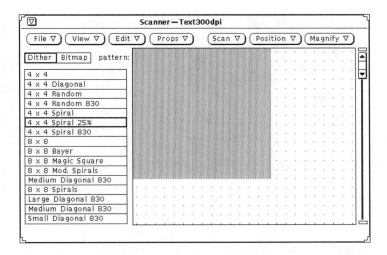

Figure 4-7   A good example of multiple control areas for one pane.

☑ Position scrollbars to the right and/or below a pane.

☑ If a large number of controls in the same window must be easily accessible, consider grouping them together in a separate command window.

For example, if the controls that are displayed to the left of the pane in Figure 4-7 were put in a separate command window, users would be able to determine their own location for the controls and the maximum amount of work area would be available for the pane.

By contrast, in the example shown in Figure 4-8, the layout is cluttered and the logic is not readily apparent. Users are forced to go to three different locations to access all of the controls, which maximizes mouse movement and forces them to remember which controls are placed in each of the three areas.

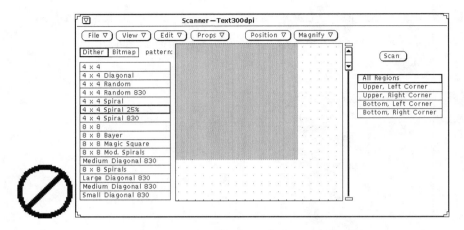

Figure 4-8   A bad example of multiple control areas for one pane.

☑︎ Use the standard layout (control area above a pane) unless you have a clear motivation for departing from it.

Suppose that you are porting a computer aided design (CAD) application from a proprietary interface. If your customers are accustomed to controls at the right, you might want to keep the same basic layout so that your customers will feel comfortable in migrating to the new version. Alternatively, you could move the controls to the left and consider providing a user-settable option that allows users to move the position of the controls to the right side of the pane.

Multiple Base Windows

Applications can be designed with multiple base windows. A mail application, for example, might devote one base window to displaying message headers and allow users to open several additional base windows for reading and composing new messages. Using multiple base windows in this case gives flexibility.

Consider the following guidelines when designing an application with multiple base windows:

☑ In most cases, base windows should be independent of one another. Each base window should have its own icon (when closed) and its own control area (when open).

☑ Consider whether it makes sense for users to quit the entire application (all of the base windows) when they quit the original base window.

If the secondary base windows are performing tasks that are integrally related to the original window, then quitting from the original window should quit the entire application. Any other base windows or icons would also be quit. On the other hand, secondary base windows that contain files that can stand alone should not be affected when users quit the original base window.

☑ If activity in one base window affects the behavior of secondary base windows, the title of the primary base window should include the word "Control."

Having a controlling base window perform actions on other base windows is an acceptable design as long as the secondary base windows can also be controlled on their own.

☑ Secondary base windows should have information in the title that shows their association with other base windows in the application. If each base window is associated with a unique function, title the base windows with the application name and the name of the function. If, however, each base window is associated with a file, include a file name and, perhaps, a number to show that each window represents another instance of the application.

Figure 4-9 shows a good example of a mail application with multiple base windows.

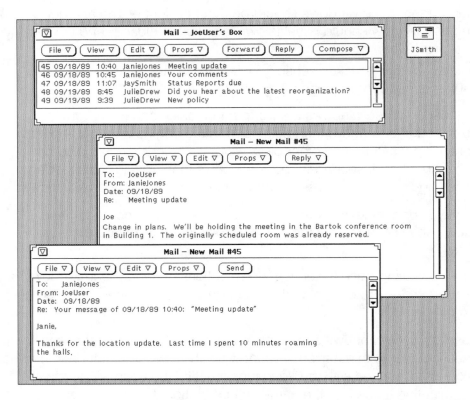

Figure 4-9   A good example of a mail application with multiple base windows.

Pop-up Windows

The OPEN LOOK UI specifies four kinds of pop-up windows that act as temporary control areas for presenting additional commands or information:

☐ Command windows allow users to specify additional information for actions such as searching, filing, or printing.

☐ Property windows give users a centralized way to view and modify the characteristics—or properties—of an object.

☐ Help windows provide users with context-sensitive help for the location under the pointer.

☐ Notices inform users of serious errors or confirm an operation that cannot be undone, such as overwriting an existing file.

This section first provides guidelines for how to organize the functionality of your application in command and property windows—the pop-up windows you will use most often. It then provides guidelines for the design and configuration of Help windows and Notices.

Command and property windows have many similarities:

☐ Multiple command and property windows can be displayed at the same time.

☐ You can associate them with your base window by including the name of the application in their titles.

☐ Typically, neither command nor property windows block input to the rest of the application. Level 2 toolkits, however, support blocking pop-up windows.

When to Use a Command Window

☑ Use command windows for operations that have options users can set to modify or specify arguments to the command.

For example, a command window for printing might allow users to specify the name of the printer, the number of copies, and the range of pages to be printed. Command windows are also used to group related operations, such as loading and saving files.

The command window shown in Figure 4-10 has text fields in which users type a string for pattern matching and replacement, settings that permit users to specify case-sensitivity and/or confirmation, and buttons to initiate the search either forward or backward.

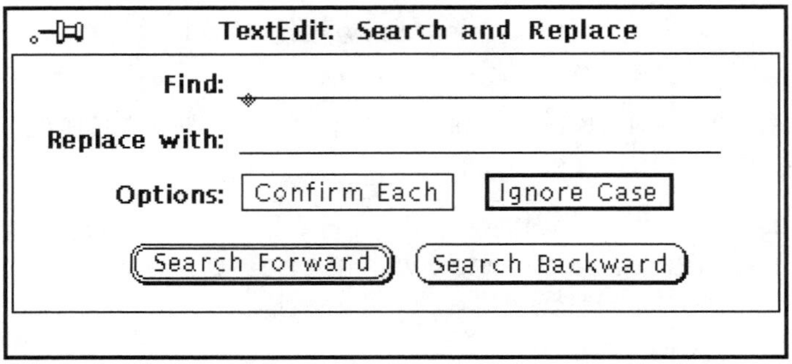

Figure 4-10 A typical command window.

When to Use a Property Window

All objects have properties. The OPEN LOOK UI specifies the properties for the workspace and for application windows. Your application specifies the properties for the objects of your application.

☑ Use property windows to give users a concise way to view and modify the characteristics of a selected object.

For example, users could select a word in a desktop publishing application and change its font, or a clock on the workspace and change its face. Figure 4-11 shows a property window for a clock.

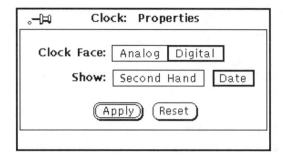

Figure 4-11   A property window for a clock.

The commands in property windows are dependent on the state of a selected object or objects: the objects have a certain state, which is accurately reflected in the settings of the property window. Users can change the state of the selected object by choosing different settings from the property window and then applying them.

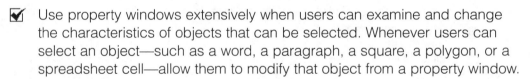 Use property windows extensively when users can examine and change the characteristics of objects that can be selected. Whenever users can select an object—such as a word, a paragraph, a square, a polygon, or a spreadsheet cell—allow them to modify that object from a property window.

Pop-up Window Configuration

Consider the following issues that are related to displaying and dismissing command and property windows and executing commands:

☐ The initial state of the pushpin
☐ The selection of contents of text fields

☐ Whether the command or property window blocks input to the application

☐ The position of execution buttons

☐ The assignment of a default button

☐ Which optional window elements to provide

The Pushpin

Each command and property window has a pushpin on the left side of the header. When the pushpin is on its side, the window is in an unpinned state. When users choose a button in the window, and the command is successfully executed, the window is dismissed. Users can choose to pin any pop-up window, keeping it on the screen for repeated operations. To do this, users click SELECT on the pushpin to pop it into the hole. The window is then pinned to the workspace, and it remains on the screen until users either unpin it or dismiss it using the Window menu.

In many cases, users want to use the command or property window for one operation and have it automatically dismissed when they successfully execute a command. If the initial state of the pushpin is unpinned, users can decide whether or not they want the pop-up window to remain on the screen. If, however, your application specifies that the pushpin for a pop-up window is pinned, it forces users to take an extra step to dismiss the window once a command has been executed.

☑ To provide users with the most flexibility, display command or property windows with the pushpin unpinned (on its side).

☑ To keep pop-up windows open by default and, consequently, to limit users' options, display the command or property windows with the pushpin pinned (in the hole).

☑ If the pop-up window does not have an execution button and the only possible action is to close the window, display the window with the pushpin pinned.

☑ When a pop-up window is pinned, the application should track the state of the selection. When there is no selection, or controls are inappropriate, make them inactive.

Text Field Selection

The text selection for the OPEN LOOK UI automatically replaces any selected text with new text as the characters are typed. When the text in a text field is selected automatically, users can type a new string immediately without needing to select the existing text.

☑ Automatically select the contents of a text field that has the caret when users display a command or property window.

☑ Allow users to clear the selection by setting the insert point anywhere within the text field (including at the end of the selection) without deleting the contents.

☑ Allow users to use the left and right cursor movement keys on the keyboard to move the insert point to the beginning or end of the text field.

☑ When there is more than one text field and the window is first displayed, always select the first field so that users can fill in the information from the top down, as they would normally.

☑ Remember the caret position if the window is pinned.

☑ Provide the standard text editing functionality for text fields, including cut/copy/paste clipboard operations.

Blocking

In Level 2 toolkits, a *blocking* pop-up window is one that prevents actions from being taken anywhere else within the domain of the parent application. The most critical time for a condition to remain unchanged by users is typically during an operation such as saving a file. Making the pop-up window busy during the execution of the operation prevents users from taking other actions in the command or property window itself. Conversely, a blocking pop-up window sets all of the other windows in the application to busy until it is dismissed.

☑ Avoid using blocking pop-up windows unless you need to ensure that users do not change the state of the application while the pop-up window is displayed.

Execution Buttons for Pop-up Windows

Buttons at the bottom of the command or property window are used to execute the function of the window or to affect the settings in the entire window. Occasionally multiple functions are represented by multiple buttons.

☑ When appropriate, provide execution buttons that execute the command specified by the button title and dismiss the pop-up window when users have not pinned the window.

☑ When appropriate, provide other buttons that affect the settings or condition of the entire pop-up window without dismissing the pop-up window regardless of whether or not the window is pinned.

Execution Buttons for Property Windows

The OPEN LOOK UI specifies the minimum set of execution buttons for property windows.

☑ Provide Apply and Reset buttons in each property window of your application.

The Apply button is the execution button for each property window. Use other buttons (such as Reset) to control the settings within the property window. Properties are not applied until users click on the Apply button. If, instead of choosing Apply, users click on Reset, any pending changes are discarded and the property window once again reflects the current state of the selected object. Figure 4-12 shows a property window with Apply and

Reset buttons. Each property window must have Apply and Reset buttons centered at the bottom of the pane.

Figure 4-12   A property window with Apply and Reset buttons.

It is important for users to count on finding the Apply and Reset buttons in the same location in every property window. Do not use a layout such as the one shown in Figure 4-13.

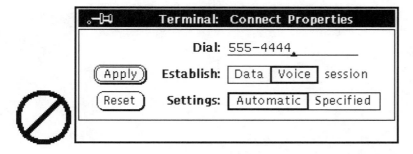

Figure 4-13   An inappropriate location for Apply and Reset buttons in a property window.

☑ Always provide an Apply button (or an Apply menu button) and Reset button centered at the bottom of the pane.

To help users determine the object that is associated with a property window, the selection for the property window is always maintained when users make a new selection anywhere on the workspace. The original selection is dimmed, but it is still active, and users can apply properties to that selection at any time by clicking SELECT on the Apply button.

For some applications, such as text editing and formatting programs, users may want to apply properties that have been set for one selection to a series of other selections. You can provide this functionality by changing the Apply button to a menu button with Original Selection and New Selection items on its menu. Figure 4-14 shows a window with an original and a new selection, and the property window for those selections. Users can change the original (dimmed) selection by moving the pointer to the Apply menu button, pressing MENU to display the Apply menu, and choosing the Original Selection item.

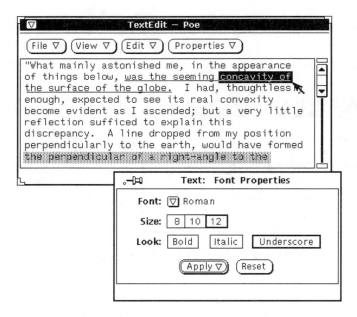

Figure 4-14 Dimmed selection feedback.

☑ Provide an Apply menu button (with Original Selection and New Selection items on the menu) instead of the Apply button when users can apply properties to another selection of the same kind in your application.

Users may want to be able to specify the properties that a new object receives when it is created. These settings represent the defaults for the object. For example, when users start typing a new document, the text uses the default properties established for text. Some applications also have the ability to make an object "plain" or "normal." This means that the settings for the object revert to the default values.

Figure 4-15 shows a property window with a Set Default button.

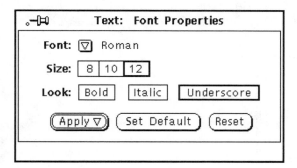

Figure 4-15   A property window with a Set Default button.

☑ Provide a Set Default button, and position it between the Apply and Reset buttons, when users can change the default settings for the property window.

Execution Buttons for Command Windows

Command windows usually have at least one execution button.

☑ Always position the button or buttons that execute the function of the command window at the bottom of the pane. The buttons that execute the command function (such as Find, Dial, or Sort), should dismiss the command window after the function is executed when the window is unpinned.

☑ Label one of the execution buttons with a label that is the same as or a derivative of the label used for the button or menu command that displayed the command window.

☑ Position any other buttons (such as Reset, Clear, and Display) that affect the command window itself above the execution buttons. Other buttons that do not invoke an action outside of the command window should not cause the window to be dismissed, regardless of the state of the pushpin.

The simple command window shown in Figure 4-16 is titled Find to match the Find window button (or window item) that users choose to display the command window. It also has a button that is labeled Find, which executes the find function.

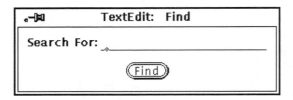

Figure 4-16 A simple single-button command window.

See Chapter 7 for more information about labeling windows and buttons. In the example shown in Figure 4-17, the Find command has been divided between two buttons, allowing users to search both forward and backward in the text.

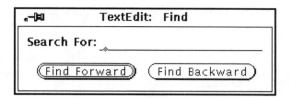

Figure 4-17 A command window with multiple buttons.

☑ When you have more execution buttons than fit comfortably in the width of the window, stack them vertically at the right of the window.

In most cases, centering the buttons at the bottom works well. However, if you have more buttons than will fit in the width of the window, it may be more compact to stack the buttons vertically, as shown in Figure 4-18.

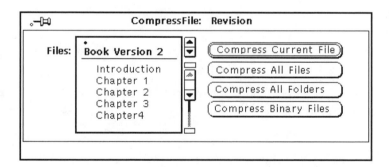

Figure 4-18 Buttons stacked on the right side of the command window.

☑ Do not mix buttons with controls representing parameters.

As you can see from the example in Figure 4-19, mixing buttons and controls in the same window can be confusing.

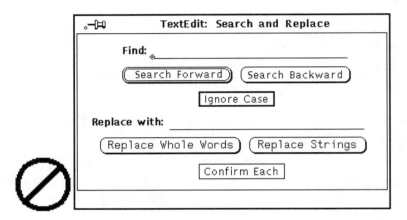

Figure 4-19   A disorderly command window.

The Default Button

Every pop-up window must have exactly one default button. In the OPEN LOOK UI, important conventions affecting the "feel" of the system are dependent on the default button:

☐ The pointer jumps to the default button when the pop-up window is displayed.

☐ The pop-up window automatically becomes the input area.

☐ The command represented by the default button is executed when users press the Default Action key on the keyboard.

For the sake of consistency, the default feedback is required even when there is only one button.

☑   Always make the Apply button (or menu button) in each property window the default button.

For command windows, your application specifies the default button. Use the following guidelines to determine which button is appropriate for the default for each command window.

☑ When there is only one execution button, make it the default, even if the command is a potentially dangerous one, such as "Delete."

☑ Position the default button as the first one in the sequence of execution buttons.

☑ When there is more than one execution button, use these guidelines to determine the default:

  ☑ The default button is the one after which the window operation is named.
  ☑ When the window has multiple operations, the default is the most common operation.
  ☑ When the window has multiple operations and no one operation can be designated as the most common, make the default the least destructive operation.

Figure 4-20 shows an example of a command window that has a good choice and location for its default button.

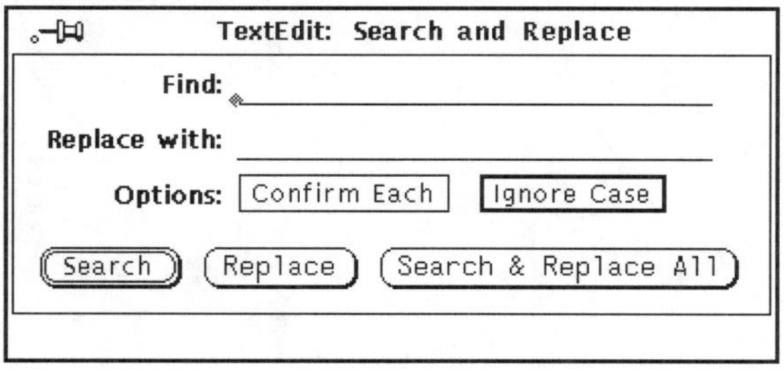

Figure 4-20 A good choice for a default button.

The default button in the example shown in Figure 4-21 is not a good choice. Users could execute the default inadvertently, altering a document in ways they did not intend. Replace All is neither the most common nor the safest operation.

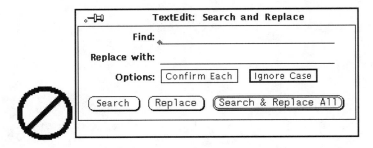

Figure 4-21   A bad choice for a default button.

Optional Window Elements for Pop-up Windows

When designing pop-up windows, you determine which optional window elements, such as resize corners and footers, are provided. Figure 4-22 shows an example of a property window with resize corners and a footer.

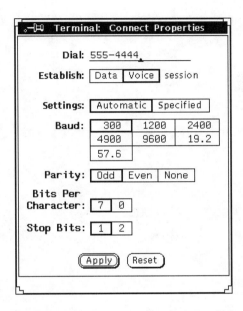

Figure 4-22 A property window with resize corners and a footer.

☑ Provide a footer for the display of status and error messages generated by the pop-up window.

☑ Provide resize corners when it makes sense (for example, when the window contains a scrolling list or scrollable text region or when the window is very large).

See "Resize Corners" later in this chapter for more information about resize corners.

Pop-up Window Layout

When arranging controls in pop-up windows, you need to choose the amount of white space for the following areas:

☐ Between all sides of the pane and the controls

☐ Between controls (horizontally and vertically)

☐ Between groups of controls (horizontally and vertically)

This section suggests guidelines for this white space. Whether you follow these guidelines or choose your own spacing, keep spacing consistent throughout your application.

☑ Always align all labels and controls with the text baseline, regardless of the height of the control.

☑ Always use consistent spacing throughout your application.

☑ Always center the execution buttons at the bottom of the pane and leave the designated amount of white space between the buttons.

The following guidelines suggest standards for spacing controls:

☑ Use a grid with the following dimensions for alignment of controls:

    ☑ For a 10-point font, use an 8-point grid.

    ☑ For a 12-point font, use a 10-point grid.

    ☑ For a 14-point font, use a 12-point grid.

    ☑ For a 19-point font, use a 16-point grid.

Figure 4-23 shows a pop-up window with a 10-point grid.

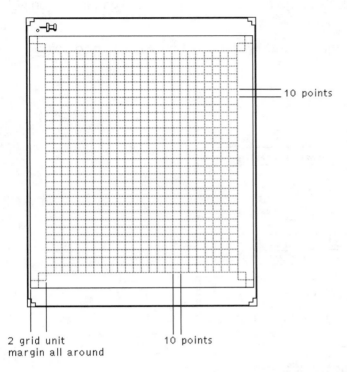

Figure 4-23 A pop-up window with a 10-point grid for aligning controls.

☑ Leave 2 grid units of white space between the left edge of the pane and the left side of the longest label.

☑ Leave 2 grid units of white space between the right side of the longest control and the right edge of the pane.

☑ Leave 1 grid unit of white space between the colon of each label and the left edge of the first control (setting, text field, slider, or check box).

☑ Leave 1 grid unit of white space between controls.

☑ Leave 2 grid units of white space between groups of controls.

☑ Center execution buttons at the bottom of the pane, leaving 1 grid unit of white space between them.

Figure 4-24 shows a property window with its controls arranged using these guidelines.

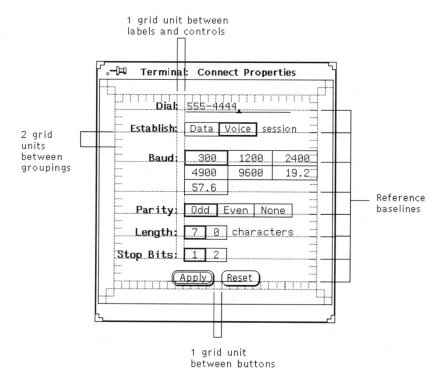

Figure 4-24 A property window with its controls arranged using the recommended grid spacing.

Arranging Controls in Command and Property Windows

☑ The basic guideline for arranging controls in command windows is to allow users to think in terms of a simple two-stage process: "This is what I want to do; now do it." The basic guideline for arranging controls in property windows is to allow users to think in terms of a simple two-stage process: "These are the properties I want to set; now set them."

You can use the full set of OPEN LOOK UI controls in pop-up windows.

☑ Arrange controls with a label on the left and the control on the right, as shown in Figure 4-25.

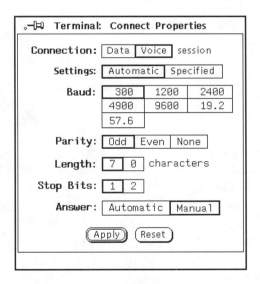

Figure 4-25 A well-organized property window.

The layout in Figure 4-25 is efficient to use. It allows users to scan the labels on the left quickly, locate the desired property, and look to the right to find the settings available for that property.

☑️ When the height of the pop-up window is a consideration, you can arrange the information in more than one column.

You can preserve the advantage of the single-column layout by arranging the columns so that users can scan the labels for each column. In the example shown in Figure 4-24, the property window has two distinct columns, each with its own set of labels. The scanning pattern is clear.

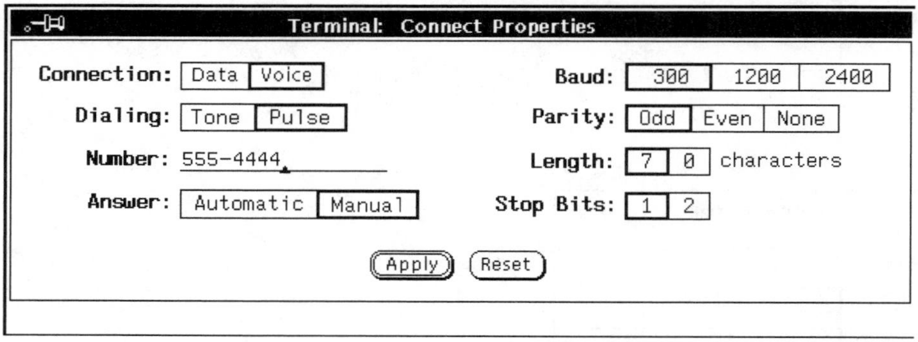

Figure 4-26 A well-organized two-column property window.

It is essential to have a logical division between the two columns. In Figure 4-26 the dialing and answering parameters are in the left column, and the modem speed and format settings are in the right column.

An improper use of multiple columns makes it difficult for users to find required controls and makes the window appear unnecessarily complicated. A worse pitfall is to try to cram as many controls as possible into a single pop-up window. The result can be a dense jumble, as shown in the example in Figure 4-27. There is not enough visual order to help users pick out the information of interest.

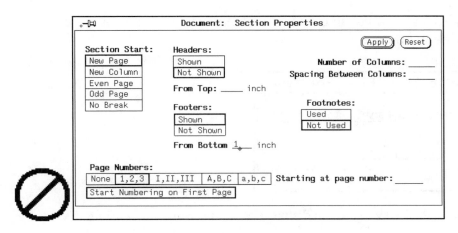

Figure 4-27 A poorly organized property window.

☑ Present one control per line with the labels on the left followed by the control on the right, when possible.

☑ Right-justify the bold labels, aligning the colons.

☑ Use a multiple-column layout to minimize the length of a pop-up window when there is a clear visual and functional distinction between columns.

☑ Put frequently used controls at the top of the pop-up window.

☑ When there is a logical sequence for choosing controls, use it to arrange the controls.

☑ Group related controls, using white space or headings.

When you are designing command windows, you need to decide whether to present controls as execution buttons or as settings. Carefully consider how to present functions in a command window. Another way to perceive this distinction is to think about buttons as verbs that do something, and settings as adverbs that modify the verbs.

☑ When you have two distinct operations for a command window, dedicate a button to each one.

Figure 4-28 shows an example of a command window with separate buttons for each operation.

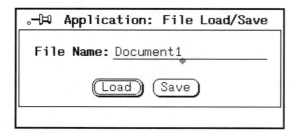

Figure 4-28 A good way to present distinct operations using separate buttons.

In the Load/Save window shown in Figure 4-29, the designer has used an exclusive setting in conjunction with a single button to determine what operation is executed. This kind of design has two drawbacks: It forces users to click twice, once on the setting to specify the desired operation and a second time on the button to execute the operation. Users could easily make an error with this design, because it is easy to perform the wrong operation.

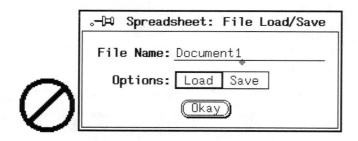

Figure 4-29 A bad way to present load and save commands.

☑ Provide settings for controls that have a state that users can set for future use without affecting the fundamental operation of the pop-up window.

☑️ Use settings only to modify the parameters of an operation, not to change the operation itself in a fundamental way.

Reading Labels as Sentences

Sometimes it works well to string the controls in a pop-up window together, treating each label as a separate clause in a single sentence. A sentence-type construction is easy to follow and eliminates the need for more lengthy labels. Figure 4-30 shows an example of a command window in which the controls read like a sentence.

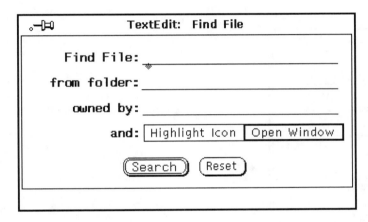

Figure 4-30 A command window in which the controls read like a sentence.

☑️ Use a sentence-type construction when there are multiple steps to a process.

Order of Controls

☑️ When you are deciding how to order the controls in a pop-up window, consider how frequently you expect each control to be used and any dependencies that may exist between controls.

☑️ Position controls so that those at the top affect those below them.

In the example shown in Figure 4-31, the controls that are related to one another are arranged in order by dependencies. When a user chooses the Filled setting for the Interiors category, the next setting contains the fill patterns. The border style and width follow the Borders setting.

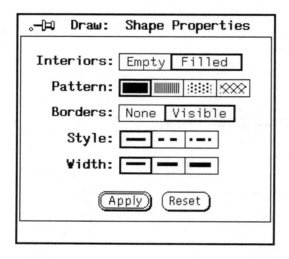

Figure 4-31 A good example of ordering of dependent controls.

The property window shown in Figure 4-32 is an example of poorly ordered controls. Users scanning down the column might think they need to choose a fill pattern, only to discover that the next category allows them to specify empty interiors.

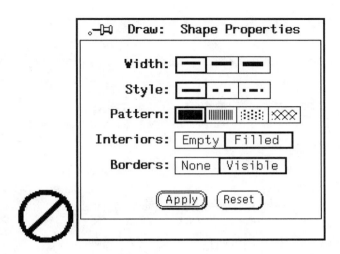

Figure 4-32 Poorly ordered controls in a property window.

☑ Arrange controls so that there is a logical sequence when some controls are dependent on others.

☑ Put the most frequently used controls toward the top of the property window.

Saving Settings Configurations

Some applications allow users to save certain combinations of settings and assign unique names to these setting combinations. An example of this is a desktop publishing application that permits users to define catalog entries for the formatting of specific types of text, such as paragraphs, headings, figures, and tables.

☑ Provide a text field in the pop-up window in which users can type the name of a user-specified group of values.

☑ For more complicated operations, provide a window button with a title such as "Save Settings As" that opens an additional pop-up window in which users can specify and name unique configurations.

When to Use a Help Window

☑ Always provide context-sensitive help for each control and area in your application.

It is your responsibility to write help messages for all the elements of your application: for each control, window, pane, and for the application as a whole. You can provide this help in two formats:

☐ *Spot help* is a brief message that is displayed in the Help window when users press the Help key. The message describes how to use the object under the pointer. Ideally, the help text is context-specific and based on the current state of the application or window.

☐ *Indexed help* is more extensive than spot help. In it users can browse through all the help screens by following links from topic to topic.

☑ Keep spot help messages brief and specific. Remember that users are trying to do something and do not want to shift their attention to read a long help message.

☑ If you want to supplement the spot help by providing an indexed help system for your application, include a button named "More" at the bottom of the Help window that displays another window containing indexed help, as shown in Figure 4-33.

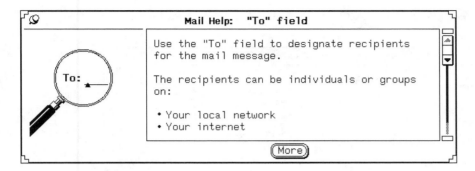

Figure 4-33   A Help window with a link to an indexed help system.

Although a single button should be sufficient, you can provide more than one button, as shown in Figure 4-34.

Figure 4-34   A Help window with more extensive options.

General Help Message

☑ Provide a general help message for your application that is displayed whenever users point at the background of the base window and press the Help key.

Figure 4-35 shows an example of a general help message.

Figure 4-35   A general help message for a mail application.

Help for Controls

The toolkit provides generic help for all the standard controls and for the background of menus. Each application must provide help for its own controls.

☑ Provide help for each control in your application, including controls on menus.

Figure 4-36 shows an example of a Help window for a message header in a mail application.

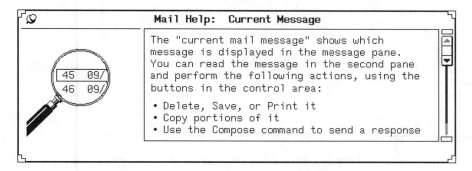

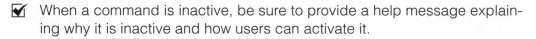

Figure 4-36 A specific help message for a control in a mail application.

Help for Inactive Controls

Frequently, users may want to operate on an object that is not selected only to find that the appropriate command is inactive.

☑   When a command is inactive, be sure to provide a help message explaining why it is inactive and how users can activate it.

Figure 4-37 shows an example of a help message for an inactive command.

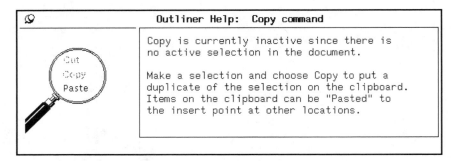

Figure 4-37   An example of help for an inactive command.

Help for Panes

☑ Provide help that describes the functionality for each pane of your application.

Figure 4-38 shows help for a pane that displays mail messages. This help text provides useful and specific information.

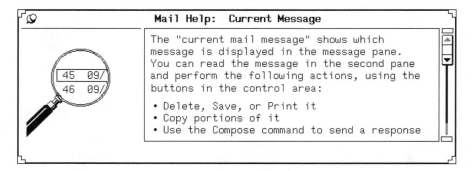

Figure 4-38   A good example of help for a pane.

If you provide help messages that convey little or no useful information, such as the one shown in Figure 4-39, users will probably stop using the help system.

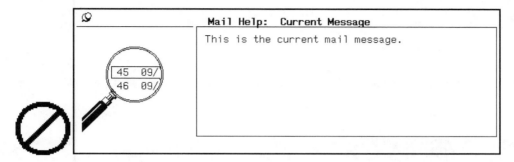

Figure 4-39 A bad example of help for a pane.

Help for Pop-up Windows

✓ Provide a help message for the background of each pop-up window that describes its functionality.

Using the Help Window to Explain Error Messages

You can use the Help window to provide detailed information that a standard-length information or error message cannot accommodate.

✓ Do not put lengthy information in an error message unless there is a useful action that can be taken based on the information you present and you know that the information will fit in the footer.

It is difficult to know the level of detail individual users require to interpret an error message correctly. For example, when you display an error message for your application, users might or might not want additional details. An expert user might already know the cause, but the novice might be overwhelmed by details. The opposite can also be true. The expert user, in an attempt to troubleshoot, might want all the details the application provides, whereas the novice might take advantage of the opportunity to learn more about the process.

☑ Keep error messages simple. When clarification is required, provide more detailed information as a help message.

Whenever your application provides additional information about error messages, find a consistent way to tell users to display the Help window. See Chapter 9 for more information about messages.

Notices

The most common use of Notices is to ask users to confirm an operation that cannot be undone, such as overwriting an existing file; to resolve an ambiguity that requires clarification before an action can be completed; or to inform users about the implications of a specific action. Notices should be used only sparingly, and not just to confirm single actions. See Chapter 9 for information about when it is appropriate for you to present Notices. The guidelines presented in the following paragraphs pertain to the visual layout and presentation of Notices.

Figure 4-40 shows a typical confirmation Notice.

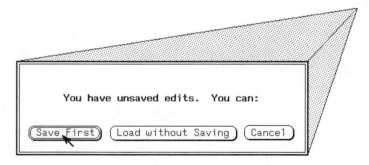

Figure 4-40 A standard confirmation Notice.

The Notice in Figure 4-41 has a Save As button. This Notice presents users with all the relevant actions they can perform.

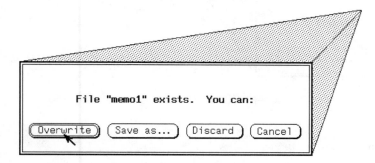

Figure 4-41 Good Notice design presents users with all the relevant actions.

Choosing the Save As button displays a pop-up window in which users can type the new file name.

☑ When users can enter a new file name for a save operation, provide a Save As window button.

The Notice shown in Figure 4-42 is not a good design. It does not present all the relevant actions as buttons in the Notice. If users want to overwrite the file, there is no problem. If, however, they want to save the file using a different name, they must cancel the Notice, display the Save As pop-up window, enter a new name, then initiate the action that displayed the Notice in the first place.

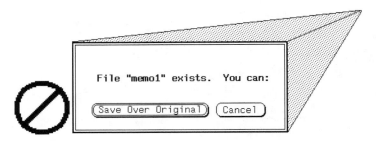

Figure 4-42 Bad Notice design does not present all the alternatives to users.

☑ Use verbs for titles in Notice buttons.

If users see a particular notice frequently, they can simply read the title on the button to choose the appropriate action. Figure 4-43 shows an example of a Notice with button titles that are verbs.

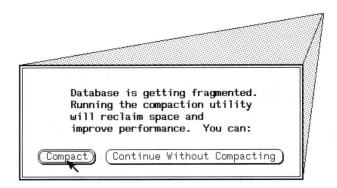

Figure 4-43 Use clearly labeled buttons on Notices.

The same information is presented in a slightly different way in Figure 4-44. Without reading the text of the Notice carefully, users cannot know what action will be performed when they choose either Yes or No. They might easily become used to clicking on the Yes button in one context and mistakenly click on the Yes button in another Notice out of habit.

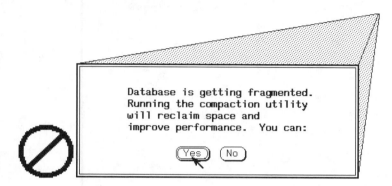

Database is getting fragmented.
Running the compaction utility
will reclaim space and
improve performance. You can:

Yes   No

Figure 4-44 Bad Notice design requires users to read the text of a Notice carefully before choosing a button.

Use the following guidelines when designing Notices:

☑ Center the buttons at the bottom of the pane.

☑ Always provide a default button, even if the Notice has only one button.

☑ Always label the button with the name of a specific command. Avoid using Yes, No, and OK buttons.

☑ Provide a button for each of the actions users can perform from a Notice.

☑ Always provide a Cancel button to allow users to dismiss the Notice without taking any other action.

☑ Keep the Notice message brief and specific.

☑ If scaling is not handled automatically by your toolkit, display the Notice in one scaling size larger than the window that originated the Notice. When the window is scaled to the largest size, use the same font size as the window.

Trade-offs for Menus, Controls, and Pop-up Windows

When deciding on the configuration for your application, you need to decide whether to provide controls directly, in menus, or in pop-up windows. This section provides guidelines for those types of tradeoffs.

Menus

Menus are ideal for presenting a small number of choices. By properly balancing the number, labels, and grouping of items in a menu, you can make it more efficient to use.

Menus versus Scrolling Regions

Scrolling lists and scrolling regions are designed to accommodate long lists of items, especially if the list can be edited and/or is likely to change in length.

☑ Do not use menus for situations in which the number of items is not fixed and can grow extremely large. Use a scrollable region—either a pane or a scrolling list—instead.

☑ Use a scrolling region instead of a menu when users can edit the list of items.

Menus versus Pop-up Windows

Menu items are chosen one at a time. After each choice, the item is executed. Menus provide an ideal method for quickly executing simple operations.

☑ When an item needs to be used in conjunction with another control, such as a text field, place the operation in a command window.

Command windows also allow users to specify multiple items. Property windows allow users to specify multiple items and then apply all of the changes at one time.

☑ When users will want to make several choices at a time, put the controls in a property or command window.

Pop-up windows let users make repeated choices without needing to display a menu each time. Such windows allow more flexibility than menus in the number, arrangement, and types of items.

Pop-up Menus

☑ Use pop-up menus in panes to complement, not replace, the menus in the control area.

☑ Design pop-up menus to contain a subset of the most commonly used commands available from the control area.

The pop-up menu shown in Figure 4-45 contains the most commonly used editing commands.

Figure 4-45 A well-designed pop-up menu.

The pane's pop-up menu is "prime real estate." Carefully consider what controls to put in it.

- ☑ Provide a title for each pop-up menu that describes the commands grouped on the menu.
- ☑ Be conservative in choosing items to include in pop-up menus.

In an application that provides many operations on several types of objects, deciding what to put in a pop-up menu is not necessarily straightforward. A problem arises when the set of legal operations varies depending on some aspect of the state of the application, such as the type of object that is selected.

- ☑ Consider putting a superset of the legal commands on the pop-up menu and selectively inactivating the commands that do not apply at any given time.
- ☑ Consider dividing the commands among two or more menus and display-ing the menu appropriate to the current state.

For example, if most operations are the same regardless of whether text or graphics are selected, use a single menu and selectively inactivate the items that do not apply.

- ☑ When the same menu items can be used no matter what object is selected, use a single pop-up menu for the pane.
- ☑ When a small percentage of the menu items are not appropriate for the selection, use a single pop-up menu that inactivates items that do not apply to the current selection.
- ☑ When the majority of menu items are not appropriate for certain selec-tions, consider having individual pop-up menus that are associated with particular objects.
    - ☑ When you use different pop-up menus, be sure to let users know by giving each menu a clear and distinct title.

☑ When the pop-up menu that is displayed is based on the selection, be sure that any items that are common from menu to menu are in the same location and order.

See Chapter 8 for more information about menus.

Determining Window Characteristics

This section discusses window characteristics, such as default, full, and minimum sizes for windows, when to use resize corners, and when to dynamically rearrange controls in the control area.

Default Window Size

You specify the default size for each window of your application. Users can change the default size for base windows and adjust the area of the window with resize corners.

☑ Make the initial size for each window large enough to accommodate the amount of data that you expect a typical user to see.

For example, suppose that a mail application is typically used to send messages of about three or four paragraphs. Displaying only a few lines by default would mean that users would have to resize the window. If, however, the application is designed primarily for transmitting binary (non-ASCII) files with short text messages attached, it might be appropriate to display only a few lines of text.

☑ Never make the default size for a base window the entire screen. Users can easily expand a base window to its full size at any time, as described in the next section.

Full Size

The OPEN LOOK UI is designed to take advantage of today's multitasking operating systems by making it easy for users to switch among several applications. Users typically have several windows open on the workspace at any given time. By choosing the Full Size item from the Window menu, users can easily expand a window to its maximum size.

☑ Choose the full size that you think is most appropriate for your application.

You specify exactly what "Full Size" means for the base window of your application. In most cases, the best interpretation is "full screen." However, for some applications, such as a text-based application in which the lines are wrapped at a certain width, it may make more sense to have Full Size expand the window to the full height of the display without changing the width.

Resize Corners

You specify whether or not a window has resize corners that allow users to adjust the area of the window.

☑ When you want to allow users to have control of the area of a window, include resize corners.

☑ Provide resize corners for any window that has a scrollable region—a scrollable pane or a scrolling list.

Resizable Base Windows

Because base windows typically contain one or more scrollable panes, they generally have resize corners.

Resizable Pop-up Windows

Pop-up windows may also contain scrollable regions. Figure 4-46 shows an example of a property window with a scrolling list and resize corners in which the resize corners may be used only to expand or contract the scrollable area. By making the window taller or shorter, users can see more or less of the contents of the scrolling list.

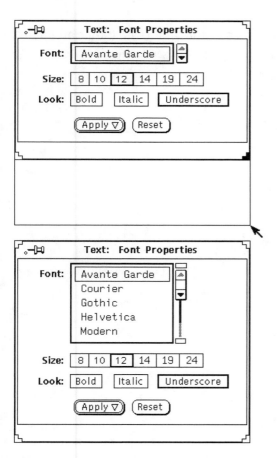

Figure 4-46 Resizable property window with a scrolling list.

Your application determines whether items inside the pane are rearranged or truncated when each window is resized.

Even if a pop-up window does not contain a scrolling list, you may want to give users the ability to resize it.

☑ If you expect controls at the top of a property window to be used most frequently, perhaps to the exclusion of others, consider providing resize corners.

When you allow users to determine the size of the windows, they can save space on the workspace by *shrinking* the window until only the desired controls are visible, as shown in Figure 4-47.

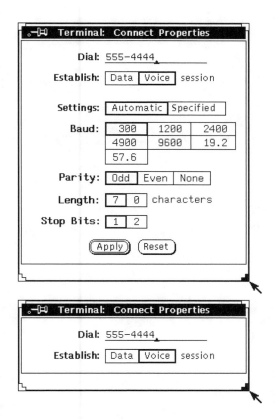

Figure 4-47 Resizing a property window to show only the top controls.

Note that the Apply and Reset buttons are no longer visible at the bottom of the pane. Users can, however, still access the associated commands from the pop-up Settings menu, as shown in Figure 4-48.

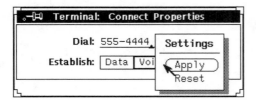

Figure 4-48 Apply and Reset items are always available from the Settings pop-up menu in a property window.

When the pop-up window is not very large, if all of its controls are roughly equal in importance, and if the window lacks scrolling regions, there is not much to be gained by resizing the window. In such cases, omit resize corners, as shown in Figure 4-49.

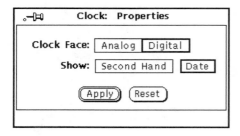

Figure 4-49 A property window without resize corners.

☑ Provide resize corners for pop-up windows only when it makes sense for users to be able to adjust the area of the window.

Resizing Windows that Have Multiple Panes

☑ When you design a window that has multiple panes and resize corners, consider how the space within the window is divided between the panes after users makes the window larger or smaller.

Suppose, for example, that a base window contains two panes. When users make the window taller, the additional height can be distributed in the following ways:

☐ Entirely in the bottom pane

☐ Entirely in the top pane

☐ Equally in the two panes

☐ In proportion to the relative sizes of the two panes. As an example, if the window has a top pane that is twice the height of the bottom pane, give the top pane two-thirds of the new height, and the bottom pane one-third of the new height.

Changing the Control Layout When a Window Is Resized

When users resize a window, a scrolling pane or a scrolling list expands or contracts. The relative positions of the controls in the control area do not automatically change.

☑ Consider dynamically changing the layout of the controls in the window when users resize it.

Rearranging the controls when the window is resized keeps all of the controls in a control area accessible when users make the window narrower. Instead of allowing the controls to be truncated, you can keep them accessible in one of the following ways:

☑ Wrap the controls onto multiple lines if you want them to be seen when the window is at its smallest size.

☑ Collapse any controls that do not fit in the new control area into a single "catch-all" menu button when it is not essential that the controls be seen at the top level.

The most general method is to take the controls that no longer fit in the control area and put them into a single menu button labeled "More." Of course, this method works only for controls such as buttons, menu buttons, and settings that can be used in menus.

☑ Place controls that cannot be displayed in menus (such as sliders and text fields) in a command window if you do not want them repositioned in the control area.

Minimum Window Sizes

The OPEN LOOK UI specifies an absolute minimum size of a pane as 16 by 16 pixels. Headers and footers keep the same height, but must always have enough width to display the Window menu button or pushpin. These minimum sizes do not provide users with a functional work area.

☑ Define a somewhat larger minimum size for each window of your application that has resize corners so that essential information always remains visible.

For example, you could specify a minimum height that offers enough room to show the header, footer, control area, and at least one line of each pane, as shown in the example in Figure 4-50.

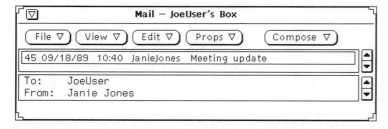

Figure 4-50 A reasonable minimum size for the base window of a mail application.

Maximum Window Sizes

You can also specify a maximum window size for each window that has resize corners. There may be times when you want to limit the maximum dimension of either the height or the width of a window, permitting users to make the window either wider or taller.

For example, when all of the controls in the property window shown in Figure 4-51 are visible, it makes little sense to permit users to expand the area of this window any farther. Users can, however, shrink the size of the window to conserve valuable screen real estate.

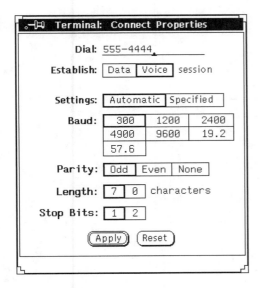

Figure 4-51   A reasonable maximum size for a property window that has a fixed number of controls.

Resizing and Splitting Panes

When your application has two or more adjacent scrollable panes, as shown in Figure 4-52, Level 2 toolkits allow users to reapportion, or resize, the area of these panes. Users can then determine how to distribute the space in the window between the panes to suit a desired usage pattern.

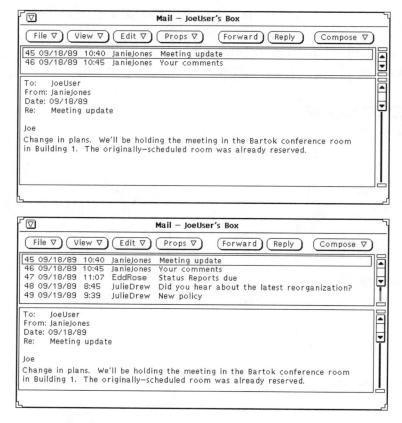

Figure 4-52   Resizable panes.

When a window has only one pane, the pane cannot be resized. You can, however, permit users to split a pane to provide multiple views into the same data. When you allow users to split panes, it makes it easier for them to make editing changes by dragging the selection from one split pane to another. Panes that users have split can always be resized in reference to one another. Figure 4-53 illustrates using one of the scrollbar cable anchors to split a pane.

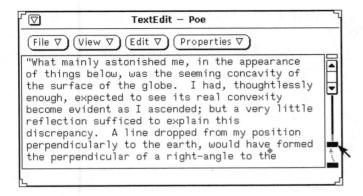

Figure 4-53 Splitting a single pane.

☑ Allow panes to be split when users can focus on multiple portions of a single object, such as a text file.

Figure 4-54 shows the two panes that result from the split, each with its own independent scrollbar.

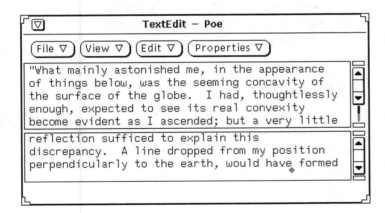

Figure 4-54 Two panes result from splitting a single pane.

155

☑️ When a pane can be split, always allow users to adjust the area between the split panes by resizing.

☑️ When the application starts with multiple panes, allow them to be resized if no essential information will be obscured.

For example, if the entire pane contains important information that users need to see, do not allow the pane size to be reduced.

☑️ If only a portion of the pane contains vital information, allow the pane to be reduced to a logical minimal size.

☑️ If you want users to have complete control over what is in view, allow a full range of pane resizing.

☑️ When a pane can be resized, make it selectable.

This means that you can provide pane-specific settings or commands.

☑️ Provide properties or commands that can be applied to a particular selectable pane.

If, for example, you have a terminal emulation tool with two panes, each representing a connection to a host, an autowrap property might be activated for one pane (by selecting the pane and applying the property from its property window) without affecting the properties of the other panes.

Scrolling with Scrollbars

When you provide scrollbars for a scrollable text region in your application, the OPEN LOOK toolkit provides most of the scrolling functionality. This section describes information you need to specify for your application when you provide scrollbars for a scrollable text region.

Defining the Scrolling Unit

The arrows on the scrollbar elevator scroll forward and backward one unit at a time. You define what constitutes a *normalization* unit for your particular application. Sometimes the decision is easy because the application has a natural unit: a line in a plain text editor, for example, or a single pixel in a drawing program.

☑ When you provide scrollbars for a pane, define the scrolling unit that provides a reasonable balance between scrolling precision and response time.

A pane might well contain objects of different sizes. For example, a desktop publishing system might mix arbitrarily sized text and graphics in a single pane. In such cases, it is not clear what the unit for scrolling should be. A smaller unit allows for greater precision, and a larger unit scrolls faster. You may want to let users decide on the trade-off between speed and precision by allowing them to redefine the scrolling unit—for example, setting it to 2 pixels instead of 1.

☑ Consider allowing users to set the scrolling unit by putting the controls for setting the scrolling unit in a property window that users can access from the Scrollbar menu or by moving the pointer onto the scrollbar and pressing the Properties key on the keyboard.

Figure 4-55 shows a Scrollbar menu with a button for setting scrolling properties.

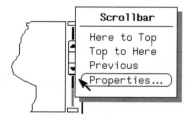

Figure 4-55   A Scrollbar menu with a button for setting properties.

Scrolling Objects of Unknown Size

In some situations, it is impossible to determine the size of the object being viewed. For example, the result of a database query might be read in only as needed. Such situations call for a slight modification of the usual scrollbar behavior.

☑ When the size of the entire object is not known, make the length of the proportion indicator represent the length of the part of the object that is known at any given point.

If users scroll to the end of the cable—either by dragging the elevator or by clicking on the end cable anchor—scroll the view to the end of the data that has already been read in. To leave the elevator at the very end would be misleading, because the view is not at the end of all the data.

☑ When the elevator is not at the end of the data, bump the elevator a few pixels upward from the bottom cable anchor to show that the view is not at the true end of the data. Put a message in the footer of the window to inform users about what is happening.

☑ When users drag the elevator again or click on the down (or right) arrow, interpret that action as a signal that users want to read in the next portion of the data.

Once the new data is read in, the scrollable object is larger, and you will need to adjust the position of the elevator accordingly.

Inactive Feedback

A scrollbar is a complex, specialized control. Like other controls, scrollbars provide users with inactive feedback by dimming one or both of the arrows in the scrollbar elevator.

When the elevator reaches either end of the cable, it cannot go any farther.

☑ Deactivate the scrollbar arrow when the elevator cannot be scrolled any farther in that direction.

Figure 4-56 shows a scrollbar with the top arrow inactive.

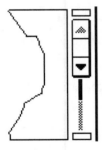

Figure 4-56   A scrollbar with one inactive arrow.

☑ Deactivate both scrollbar arrows when the data being viewed fits entirely within the viewing pane.

Figure 4-57 shows a horizontal and vertical scrollbar with inactive scrolling buttons.

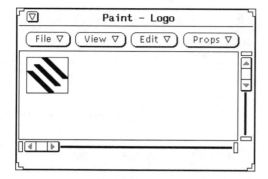

Figure 4-57   Scrollbars with both arrows inactive.

Adding to the Scrollbar Menu

The basic Scrollbar menu contains items that scroll the line next to the pointer to the top of the pane, the line at the top to where the pointer is, and back to the previous scrolling position.

☑ Enhance the basic Scrollbar menu with other features to enhance scrolling productivity in your application.

For example, you can use the Scrollbar menu to let users set marks at arbitrary places in the scrolling object. Using these marks, users can scroll directly to places in the data that they choose. You can do this in several ways:

☑ When you allow only one marked location, add an item to the Scrollbar menu titled "Set Mark."

Choosing this item sets a marker (which may be invisible to users or visible but not printable) at the insert point in the document. Add another item titled "Go To Mark" that automatically scrolls the contents to the set mark location.

☑️ If you want to permit users to set more than one mark, add additional items, assigning each mark a unique number.

☑️ Consider displaying a command window that allows users to assign names to each of the marks.

The customized names could be added as items to the Scrollbar menu, as shown in Figure 4-58.

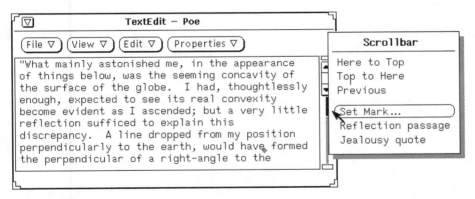

Figure 4-58 Adding commands to the basic Scrollbar menu.

Page-oriented Scrollbars

Level 2 toolkits provide page-oriented scrollbars that display the current page number in a box next to the scrollbar elevator when users move the pointer onto the drag area and press SELECT. Figure 4-59 shows a page-oriented scrollbar. Dragging the pointer interactively updates the page number that is displayed to the left of the scrollbar elevator.

Figure 4-59 A page-oriented scrollbar.

☑ When your application organizes data logically into pages, provide page-oriented scrollbars.

☑ Consider displaying the page number at the right of the footer as a state message.

See Chapter 9 for more information about state messages.

Panning and Automatic Scrolling

Level 2 toolkits provide two ways of scrolling without a scrollbar—panning and automatic scrolling. Panning allows users to scroll small distances without having to move the pointer to the scrollbar. Automatic scrolling ensures that the input area is visible during data entry and tracks pointer movement when the pointer is being dragged. When users are copying or moving data by dragging, automatic scrolling permits them to copy or move the data to an area that is not visible in the pane when the operation is initiated.

☑️ Use the panning modifier key provided by your toolkit if you implement your own panning functionality.

☑️ Provide panning and automatic scrolling when the operations are important to your application, even if they are not provided as part of your toolkit.

Interacting with Other Applications Using Drag and Drop

The OPEN LOOK File Manager provides functionality for dragging icons representing files and dropping them onto other windows, icons, or glyphs. For example, users can print files by selecting several data file icons, dragging them onto a printer icon, and dropping them. The term "drop" is a shortcut for the completion of a move or duplicate operation. First users select an object; then they initiate a move or duplicate by pressing the SELECT mouse button and dragging the pointer. When the hot spot of the pointer is at an appropriate place and users release the SELECT mouse button, the object is "dropped" into the new location.

☑️ Consider supporting the following actions that will permit your application to interact with a file manager and other applications that use the drag and drop method.

Format of Acceptable Data for Dropping

The data that users drag to your application may be either objects that they selected or an icon. When the data is represented as an icon, the application itself is not moved or duplicated into your application. Instead, dropping an icon onto another application moves or duplicates the data contained in that application.

☑️ Accept data that is represented as an icon as well as selected objects.

Receiving Dropped Data in the Base Window

☑ When users drop an object onto the background of the base window, load the data into your application, overwriting any previous content. If the old data in the window has not been saved, display a Notice so that users can save the old data if they want to.

☑ When users drop an object onto the pane of a base window, insert the data at the hot spot of the move or duplicate pointer.

☑ If the new object is not of the same type as the objects in the destination pane, either insert the object inside a frame or convert it to a format that is acceptable by the pane.

If, for example, users drop a PostScript graphic object into a bitmap paint tool, convert the object to bitmap format. As part of its import and export functionality, your application may have filters that can be used for processing data that is dropped into the application: Many word processing applications have filters to convert text from one text editor format to another.

☑ If your application cannot decide how to handle the data format, display a Notice that lists the available options.

Receiving Dropped Data on the Icon

☑ Handle data that is dropped onto the icon of your application in the same way as data that is dropped onto the background of the base window: load the data into the application, overwriting any previous content. If the old data in the window has not been saved, display a Notice so that users can save the old data if they want to.

For example, if the data file is dropped onto the icon of a text editor application, the data should be loaded into the application, overwriting any previous text.

☑️ Consider providing a user preference to allow users to decide if it is appropriate for your application to open an icon automatically when it receives dropped data.

☑️ When your application is the recipient of a drop, but cannot accept moved data, display a Notice with Duplicate and Cancel buttons that allow users to proceed, change the operation to duplicate, or cancel.

For example, to safeguard loss of data in printing operations, a printing application may accept only files that are duplicated. If your application has any such restrictions, display a Notice to allow users to cancel the operation or change it from move to duplicate.

When to Display Notices

Your application should always display a Notice when there is a potential loss of data or ambiguity of an operation. The four circumstances for displaying Notices when using drag and drop operations are:

☐ When the application cannot accept the data

☐ When data at the destination will be overwritten without being saved

☐ When there are options for converting the data to a different format

☐ When a destination cannot accept a move operation, but a duplicate is acceptable

Source and destination applications should not try to second-guess whether or not users really want to move a file. Move should always initiate a move, and duplicate should always make a copy of the source data. There may, however, be instances in which moving data is not appropriate for a destination application. If a move operation is perceived as inappropriate, always display a Notice that allows users to complete the move if they choose to do so.

5

DATA ENTRY, SELECTION, AND MANIPULATION

Introduction

When you have decided on the basic configuration of your application—the equivalent of the number, size, and location of rooms in the house—the next step is for you to decide how users interact with the data. The OPEN LOOK Graphical User Interface specifies how users select and operate on objects such as text and graphics. Your application should always conform to the specified selection actions and feedback. This chapter provides guidelines for additional selection functionality you can add.

This chapter describes the following functionality:

☐ Selecting data
☐ Using the selection
☐ Keyboard functions

Selecting Data

☑ Always use the OPEN LOOK UI-specified selection mechanism for text and graphics.

Selection Feedback

In the select-then-operate model, users first choose data in an application, then they choose a command that operates on that data. The chosen data is called the *selection*.

Text

When users select text, it displays *highlighted*, as shown in Figure 5-1.

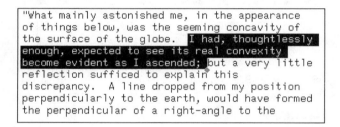

Figure 5-1   Text selection feedback.

If users select text and then either type new text or paste text from the clipboard, the selected text is deleted automatically. Users can, therefore, quickly replace text by selecting it and then typing new text.

In fact, the OPEN LOOK UI makes it easy for users to replace text in a text field by automatically selecting it when the insert point is moved into a text field.

Multi-click Selection for Text

One easy shortcut you can provide users for selecting text is to define a hierarchy for multiple clicks of the SELECT mouse button, as follows:

☐ Single-clicking sets the insert point but does not select any characters.

☐ Double-clicking selects a word.

☐ Triple-clicking selects either a line, a sentence, or a paragraph.

☐ Quadruple-clicking selects either a paragraph (if not part of a triple-click selection), a page, or the entire document.

☑ Define a multi-click hierarchy for text in your application.

Users can set the time between clicks for multi-click operations from the Workspace Properties window. Keep in mind that single- and double-clicks are easy for most users; however, many users may find triple- and quadruple-clicking operations difficult to perform.

Extend the multi-click selection to include wipe-through selections, if this functionality is not provided by your toolkit.

☑ When users select an object or text with the multi-click technique and then extend the selection (by dragging, or by moving the pointer and clicking ADJUST), your application should grow and shrink the selection by the originally defined increment.

For example, if users click SELECT and then press SELECT and drag the pointer, the selection should change by character increments. If users double-click SELECT to select a word and then press SELECT and drag the pointer, the selection should change by word increments.

Graphics

When users select a graphic object, you can provide one of three kinds of visual feedback for the selected object, as shown in Figure 5-2:

□ Thickening the border of the selected graphic

□ Highlighting (with reverse video) the selected graphic

□ Displaying grab handles for the selected graphic

Unselected **With border** **Highlighted** **With grab handles**

Figure 5-2   Examples of different types of graphics selection feedback.

☑ Thicken the border or highlight the graphic object when it has a perma-
nent fixed size. Thicken the border in a color implementation to maintain
the color of the object.

☑ Use grab handles when the object does not have an application-fixed
size and users can resize it.

Typically, eight grab handles are positioned at each corner and at the
midpoint of each side. Users resize the object by dragging the handles. The
corner grab handles can be dragged in any direction, but the side grab
handles move in one dimension only. Figure 5-3 shows a triangle (left) that
has been stretched horizontally (right).

 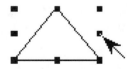

Figure 5-3   Grab handles can be used to stretch an object.

Window and Icon Selection Feedback

Windows and icons are also graphic objects that can be selected and operated on directly or from a Window Controls pop-up. The border thickens to show selection for windows and icons. Figure 5-4 shows selected and unselected windows and icons.

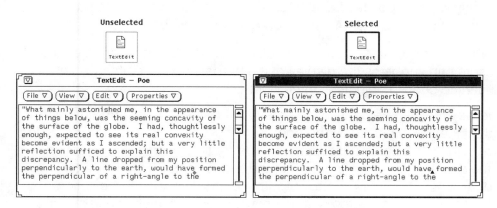

Figure 5-4   Selection feedback for windows and icons.

Multi-click Selection for Graphic Objects

Some applications have graphic objects structured into a hierarchy with smaller objects contained within larger objects. In such cases, users may need to be able to select successively higher levels in the hierarchy by multi-clicking. A single click selects the object under the pointer, double-clicking selects the object that contains the one under the pointer, and triple-clicking selects the object at the next highest level. Quadruple-clicking selects all objects. Users set the multi-click timeout factor (the maximum length of time between clicks—the release of the mouse button and the next press) from the Workspace Properties window.

☑   Define a multi-click hierarchy for graphic objects in your application.

"Select Parent" Command

Many word processing or desktop publishing applications allow users to select *frames* around text or graphics. Selecting these frames can be difficult. The frame borders are typically not shown. When they are shown, the borders are usually only a single point wide and are, therefore, difficult to select accurately with the pointer. Level 2 toolkits provide a target pointer to help users see when the pointer is on the border of a pane or a frame.

☑ When your application contains objects embedded in other objects and users can suppress the display of the borders, provide an easy way for users to choose objects at each level.

One way to help users select a frame is to provide a Select Parent command on the Edit menu or on the pop-up menu for the pane. Choosing Select Parent selects the frame containing the current text or graphics selection.

In the example shown in Figure 5-5, the text is contained within a text frame (the dotted box), which is contained within a graphics frame (the solid box). Initially, some text is selected (left). Choosing Parent selects the text frame (middle). Choosing Select Parent again selects the graphics frame (right).

Figure 5-5   Selection feedback for embedded objects.

Selecting Data in Tables

When you design your application to present data in tables, use the conventions described in this section.

☑ Indicate that a cell or group of cells is selected by thickening the cell border.

Figure 5-6 shows a table with a single cell selected.

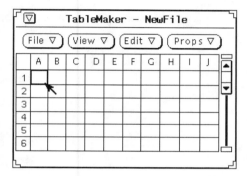

Figure 5-6   A table with a single cell selected.

☑ Permit users to select an arbitrary range of cells with a bounding box.

A bounding box is created when users press SELECT and drag the pointer. All cells falling completely within the bounding box are selected, as shown in Figure 5-7.

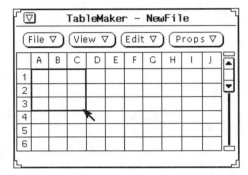

Figure 5-7   A table with a range of cells selected.

☑ Permit users also to select a range of cells by clicking SELECT on one cell and then moving the pointer to another cell and clicking ADJUST to add it to the selection.

☑ Permit users to click SELECT on the header of a row to select all the cells in the row.

Figure 5-8 shows a table with a row of cells selected.

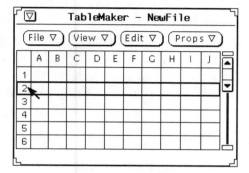

Figure 5-8   A table with a row of cells selected.

☑ Permit users to click SELECT on the header of a column to select all the cells in the column.

Figure 5-9 shows a table with a column of cells selected.

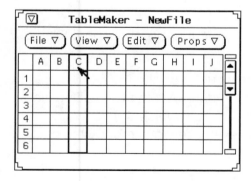

Figure 5-9   A table with a column of cells selected.

Quick Operations

Level 2 implementations provide two additional operations called *Quick Move* and *Quick Duplicate*, which allow users to move or copy text to the insert point in a single step without affecting the selection or the clipboard.

To move text to the insert point (Quick Move), users press the Cut key, select the desired text, and release the Cut key. To copy to the insert point (Quick Duplicate), users press the Paste key, select the desired text, and release the Paste key.

☑ Provide both quick operations whenever possible.

Quick operations provide an efficient way for users to perform the common operations of moving or duplicating existing text to the current insert point. They can also be used for situations in which text ordinarily cannot be selected. Ordinarily, pressing SELECT and dragging over the text in the window footer drags the window rather than selecting the text. Using the Quick Duplicate operation allows users to copy the text in the header or footer. For example, a user might want to copy an error message that is displayed in the footer and include it in a mail message to facilitate trouble-shooting.

☑ Implement Quick Duplicate operations for your application, particularly for text that cannot be selected.

Ordinarily, dragging SELECT over an icon would drag the icon. Suppose users had a clock icon that also displayed the date. Without Quick Duplicate, they could not select the date from the clock icon. If Quick Duplicate is implemented for the date on the clock, however, users could copy the date into another window, as shown in Figure 5-10.

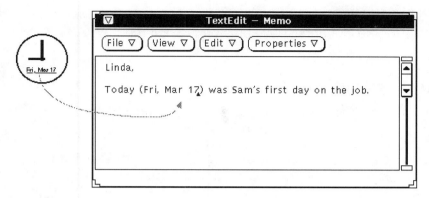

Figure 5-10   Copying the date from a clock using Quick Duplicate.

Operating on Selected Text

The basic way to operate on text is with the clipboard operations *Cut, Copy,* and *Paste*. These commands should always be available as part of the core functions provided from the keyboard. In addition, you can provide these commands as part of your application design.

☑ Always use the OPEN LOOK clipboard for Cut, Copy, Paste commands.

☑ Always provide Cut, Copy, and Paste commands from the keyboard.

☑ Always provide Cut, Copy, and Paste commands on the Edit menu in the control area of the base window, and on an Edit pop-up menu for the pane.

Command windows provide a useful mechanism for text operations. For example, your application may provide a command window that permits users to search for and replace text strings in a word processing application.

☑ Consider extending clipboard functionality by allowing users to choose whether to overwrite or append to the contents of the clipboard. One way to provide this functionality is to provide a submenu with Overwrite and Append items for the Cut and Copy items on the edit menu.

Changing Text Properties

Another common way users operate on selected text is to change its properties by modifying settings in a property window.

☑ Provide a property window to permit users to set properties such as font types and point sizes for a word processing application.

Smart Word Handling

Smart word handling refers to the correct handling of the white space on either side of text that is moved or duplicated. A word is usually defined as any sequence of alphanumeric characters. Sometimes some special characters, such as a dash (–) or an underscore (_), are included.

☑ Use the definition of a word that makes the most sense in the context of your application.

☑ When users move or duplicate text, precede and follow the words with the correct number of spaces.

The examples that follow offer some guidelines for handling white space.

1 User selects one or more words to be deleted or moved to a new location.
2 User initiates the delete or move operation.
3 The application automatically removes one of the spaces on either end of the deleted words, leaving a single space in place of the deleted text, as shown in Figure 5-11.

How malicious is my fortune that that I must repent to be just!

How malicious is my fortune that I must repent to be just!

Figure 5-11 Deleting one or more words leaves only one space.

1 User selects a word or words at the end of a sentence (not including the punctuation mark).

2 User initiates a delete or move operation.

3 The application automatically deletes the space that preceded the selected words, positioning the punctuation mark immediately following the new last word in the sentence, as shown in Figure 5-12.

How malicious is my fortune that I must repent to be just okay!

How malicious is my fortune that I must repent to be just!

Figure 5-12 Deleting words at the end of a sentence.

1 User selects one or more words to be moved or copied to a new location between two words.

2 User initiates the move or copy operation.

3 The application automatically inserts an additional space, so that the words are preceded and followed by a space, as expected. Figure 5-13 shows an example.

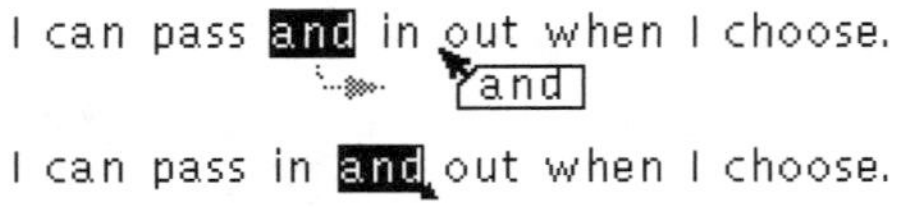

I can pass **and** in out when I choose.

I can pass in **and** out when I choose.

Figure 5-13 Moving or duplicating words to a new location.

1 User selects one or more words.

2 User moves or copies the selected words to the beginning of a sentence.

3 The application automatically inserts a space after the moved or copied words, as shown in Figure 5-14.

Starting Point **The**

The Starting Point

Figure 5-14 Moving or duplicating words to the beginning of a sentence.

1 User selects one or more words.

2 User moves or copies the selection to the end of a sentence (after the last word but before the period).

3 Application automatically inserts a space before the words, as shown in Figure 5-15.

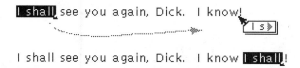

Figure 5-15 Duplicating words to the end of a sentence.

Keyboard Use

The number of keys on a keyboard is limited. To expand the functionality of the keyboard, the OPEN LOOK UI allows keys to be modified, providing a new function when the user presses more than one key at a time.

Core Operations

☑ Always implement the core set of operations from the keyboard for your application. Support these functions as thoroughly as possible.

All OPEN LOOK systems provide the following set of core functions from the keyboard:

- ☐ Cut/Copy/Paste
- ☐ Help
- ☐ Properties
- ☐ Stop
- ☐ Undo

☑ Always implement core function keys in a hardware-independent way, as provided by your toolkit. Proper implementation permits users to change the default assignments for these keys from the Workspace Properties window.

Keyboard Mappings

Some keyboards have dedicated keys for some or all core operations. In the absence of a dedicated key, the OPEN LOOK system maps the operation to a key combination such as Control-U for Undo. Users can change the mapping at any time from the Workspace Properties window.

Overriding Keyboard Mappings

It is important for users to be able to invoke the core operations in the same way throughout the system. An application might, however, have a legitimate need to override the global mappings for a particular core function. For example, the default mapping for Cut is Control-C. If you are developing a terminal emulator, you may need to interpret Control-C as Cancel and provide an alternate mapping for Cut.

☑ Do not override the global mappings unless there is a clear need to do so.

☑ If the need to override global mappings exists, provide a mode that allows users to toggle between the standard mappings and the unique mappings of the application.

☑ When the application is in "override" mode, use the right side of the footer (the state/mode message area) to notify users.

The following sections describe each of the core operations.

Cut/Copy/Paste

The standard clipboard operations are as follows:

☐ Cut deletes the selection and puts a copy of it on the clipboard.

☐ Copy copies the selection to the clipboard without deleting it.

☐ Paste inserts the contents of the clipboard at the current insert point.

☑ Always use the OPEN LOOK clipboard for Cut/Copy/Paste operations.

Help

Display a Help window for the object under the pointer.

Properties

Display the property window for the selected object.

Stop

Cancel the current operation. Stop has two functions:

☐ To prematurely stop an action that is awaiting completion. For example, graphics packages often have drawing modes for complex objects. Many programs continue drawing a polygon (following the mouse movement) until the shape is closed. Pressing Stop would terminate the drawing.

☐ To cancel an operation that may take a long time. Examples include a database query or the repagination of a document.

The Stop operation applies to the object that is under the pointer when users click the appropriate key or key combination.

☑ If stopping the process has serious ramifications—such as wasting hours of processing time that took place prior to the requested stop, a file's integrity being lost, or the stopping action itself possibly taking a while—display a Notice that states the situation and asks users whether to stop or proceed.

Undo

Undo the last operation that took place in the window containing the current input area. Increments of undo include undoing the previous function (invoking a command or setting) and undoing the previous entry (input that occurred subsequent to the previous caret relocation based on pointer and/or keyboard repositioning).

☑ As a minimum, implement one level of undo so that, if users invoke Undo twice in succession, the first undo reverses the effect of the most recent operation, and the second undo restores the effect of the operation.

You can also implement multi-level undo, in which successive invocations of undo reverse successive operations, beginning with the most recent and working backward.

Dragging Operations

There is another set of operations that users invoke by pressing a modifier while dragging an object with the pointer. Such modifiers are called *dragging modifiers*. They include:

☐ Set Menu Default

☐ Constrain

☐ Duplicate

☐ Pan

The toolkit typically implements Set Menu Default. The other three operations—Constrain, Duplicate, and Pan—are your responsibility to implement when using a Level 1 toolkit. Because these operations are common, it is important that users be able to perform them in the same way from application to application.

If you provide Constrain, Duplicate, or Pan operations in your application, consider mapping Constrain to Shift, Duplicate to Control, and Pan to a third modifier, such as Alt or Meta.

Keyboard Mappings

As they can map the core operations, users can set the dragging modifier keys globally, for all applications, from the Workspace Properties window.

☑ To make remapping possible, use the appropriate event as defined by your toolkit.

☑ Do not hard-code the operation to a particular modifier.

The following sections describe the dragging modifiers.

Set Menu Default

The Set Menu Default modifier allows users to specify which menu control is the default. This function is typically implemented by your toolkit.

Constrain

Pressing the Constrain modifier while dragging constrains the dragging to a single axis. Constraining is useful in many contexts, particularly in drawing and painting applications.

The OPEN LOOK UI defines a *damping factor*, which is the number of pixels users can move the pointer before a drag is initiated.

☑ Constrain the movement in the direction of movement of the pointer after the damping factor is reached.

For example, if the damping factor is 6 pixels and users move the pointer 5 pixels to the right and 8 pixels upward, ignore the 5 pixels of horizontal motion, which do not exceed the damping factor, and constrain the movement to the vertical direction, which does exceed the damping factor.

☑ Allow users to press and release the Constrain modifier at any time during the drag operation, thereby activating and deactivating the constraint.

Duplicate

If users press the Duplicate modifier, the result of dragging an object is to create a copy of the object in the new position, leaving the original object and the contents of the clipboard unchanged.

Note that the term "duplicate" is used instead of "Copy" to avoid confusion with the standard copy to the clipboard operation.

Pan

Panning is a way of scrolling without using scrollbars. When users press the Pan modifier, the contents of the pane become, in effect, "glued" to the pointer. As long as users keep pressing the Panning modifier, moving the pointer causes the entire contents of the pane to move in lock-step with the pointer. When the contents have been dragged to the edge of the pane, the pane scrolls automatically.

Keyboard Accelerators

A *keyboard accelerator* is a key or sequence of keys on the keyboard that allows users to perform specific functions without using a menu. The core operations described previously are global keyboard accelerators that apply across applications. This section offers guidelines for providing local keyboard accelerators that are specific to your application. You set the default values for any keyboard accelerators. However, users should be able to customize the accelerators with settings you provide in the application-specific property window.

For example, in addition to the global keyboard accelerators such as Cut, Properties, and Undo, a word processing application might provide specific functions, such as capitalization and paragraph indentation. These application-specific functions should be provided in a keyboard category of the application properties. Global properties are determined only by the controls in the Workspace Properties window.

User Mapping of Keyboard Accelerators

☑ Provide a property window for application-wide properties with a Keyboard category from which users can assign the keys and modifiers to use for keyboard accelerators.

This is necessary for two reasons:

☐ To provide device independence

☐ To allow users to specify preferred accelerators

For example, because not all keyboards have an Alt key, it clearly does not work to hard-wire your accelerators to use Alt. By letting users choose from the commonly available modifiers, such as Alt and Control, you will isolate your application from such hardware dependencies.

Mnemonic Keys versus Function Keys

The phrase *mnemonic key* refers to using the key that represents the first letter of a command in conjunction with a single modifier, such as Control or Shift, as a keyboard accelerator. For example, Control/P could mean Print, or Control/S could mean Save.

Mnemonic keys are generally better than dedicated function keys for several reasons:

☐ The number and location of function keys varies from keyboard to keyboard.

☐ Some keyboards do not have any function keys.

☐ Touch typists prefer to keep their hands on the standard keyboard.

Good examples of common mnemonic functions are:

☐ Control/Q for Quit

☐ Control/P for Print

☐ Control/W for Close Window

☐ Control/S for Save

Modifier Keys

☑ Consistently use one modifier as a "command" modifier.

If possible, limit the assignment of mnemonic accelerators to one specific modifier, such as Control. If the core functions are bound to a modifier instead of function keys, then try to use the same modifier. For example, if the toolkit binds COPY to Control/C, then try to limit the assignment of your functions to Control plus one other key.

☑ Assign consistent meaning to additional modifier keys.

If using additional modifiers becomes necessary, try to assign a consistent meaning to those modifiers. For example, in a text-editing application, you might use Alt to modify commands that operate directly on text and Control to access global editing commands such as search, save, and quit. Dividing functions into categories in this way greatly increases their mnemonic value.

☑ Avoid chording (pressing multiple keys simultaneously) of multiple modifiers.

Instead of requiring users to press two or more modifier keys at the same time, such as Control-Shift/H or Control-Meta/P, assign a sequence of keys that provides the same functionality.

☑ Use "synthetic modifiers" if you need to expand the set of available modifiers.

☑ If the set of available modifiers is not adequate for the number of functions in your application, consider synthesizing additional modifiers.

For example, few keyboards have a Hyper key. The effect of typing Hyper/Q can be achieved by combining other modifier sequences to generate the appropriate command. If you assign Control/X to Hyper, the sequence Control/X, Control/Q generates a Hyper/Q.

Consider defining a modifier key for backspace to make it easy for users to delete a word and the space following it without requiring an extra keystroke. Users press the modifier key and Backspace together to delete a word and the space immediately following it in one step.

Numbered Accelerators

☑ When lists of commands or items are involved, it is appropriate to use numbers instead of letters as accelerator keys.

When a spelling checker encounters an unknown word, for example, it presents alternative spellings from which users can choose, as shown in Figure 5-16.

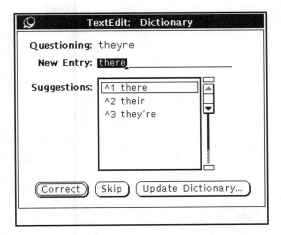

Figure 5-16 Numbered accelerators for a scrolling list.

The alternate spellings are presented in the scrolling list. Clicking on the Use Entry button causes the current item in the list ("there" in the above example) to be substituted for the misspelled word.

6

CHOOSING AND USING CONTROLS

Introduction

Controls are like light switches and doorknobs. Switches turn things on and off and doorknobs allow you to access other rooms in the house. The controls you choose for each of your windows provide similar functions for your application.

This chapter provides guidelines for choosing controls both for the base window and for other parts of your application. The final section of this chapter describes the visual feedback for OPEN LOOK Graphical User Interface controls.

The Control Area of a Base Window

As mentioned in Chapters 2 and 4, the base window of your application should contain frequently used controls and features of the application so that users can find them easily. This section provides guidelines for a standard control area of a base window.

☑ Always start the controls in your base window control area with File, View, Edit, and Properties menu buttons, unless your application functionality does not fit neatly into one of these categories.

☑ Group the File, View, Edit, and Properties menu buttons together at the left of the control area.

Figure 6-1 shows a control area with standard File, View, Edit, and Properties menu buttons.

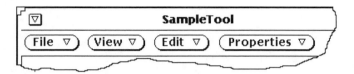

Figure 6-1   A control area with the standard File, View, Edit, and Properties menu buttons.

☑ Provide white space between these four standard buttons and any other controls that you put in the control area of the base window.

☑ If you omit one (or more) of the standard buttons, leave a gap equal to the amount of white space that is used to separate groups of buttons where the button would normally appear. This helps users to associate the position of the button with its function, regardless of whether the other standard buttons are provided.

☑ Pop-up windows should never have File, View, or Edit menu buttons or any other menu buttons that are found in the control area of the base window.

Individual items from the menus of these buttons are, however, appropriate. A Print button, for example, can be used in a pop-up window.

The following sections provide general criteria to help you decide what to put in each of the standard menus, specific suggestions for contents of the standard menus, and a typical example of each menu.

The File Menu

☑ Use the File menu to present controls that are related to loading and storing files, creating new files, and printing.

A typical File menu is shown in Figure 6-2.

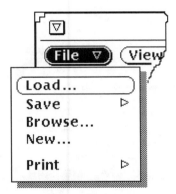

Figure 6-2   A typical File menu structure.

Load and Save Operations

Most applications permit users to load data, edit it, and save the changes. You can provide Load and Save functions as separate items on the File menu or combine them into a Load/Save window item.

When you provide Load and Save as separate items, make Load a window item. Choosing the Load window item displays a command window in which users enter the name of the object to be loaded. This command window typically has a text field and a command button labeled Load, as shown in Figure 6-3.

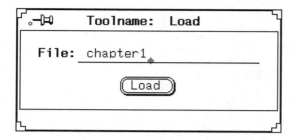

Figure 6-3   A typical Load command window.

☑ Make Load the default item for the file menu when you provide Load and Save as separate items on the menu.

☑ Always display a Notice when users initiate a load that would overwrite a file that has not been saved or that has unsaved edits.

Display Save as a menu item. The Save submenu should have at least the following items:

☐ Document

☐ Options . . .

Choosing Document saves the file using the current settings. Choosing Options opens a command window in which users can type a new name.

☑ Provide load and save operations in the same command window when users frequently load files and save them again using the same file name, and when it is important to conserve screen real estate.

When you provide a Load/Save window item, choosing it displays a command window in which users enter the name of the object to be loaded or to be saved. This command window typically should have a text field and command buttons labeled Load and Save, as shown in Figure 6-4.

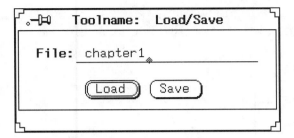

Figure 6-4   A typical Load/Save command window.

☑ Make Load/Save the default for the File menu, because it is the most common filing activity performed by users.

☑ Make Load the default button for the command window when Load and Save are combined.

☑ When appropriate, supplement or replace the Load and Save buttons in the command window with other functions specific to your application.

☑ Consider providing an exclusive hierarchical scrolling list as part of the Load window.

Figure 6-5 shows an example of a Load window with an exclusive hierarchical scrolling list. Users can either type the name of a file or choose a name from the scrolling list.

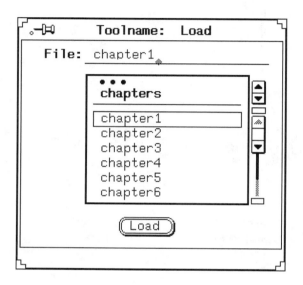

Figure 6-5   A Load command window with an exclusive hierarchical scrolling list.

☑ Consider providing a nonexclusive hierarchical scrolling list and settings that allow users to select more than one file for loading and decide whether to load the files in the same or different windows

Figure 6-6 shows an example of a Load window with a nonexclusive hierarchical scrolling list and settings that specify whether the file is to be loaded into a new window or into the current one. When users can choose more than one file, the Same window setting appends the selected files and loads them all in the same window. When users choose the New window setting, a new base window is opened for each selected file.

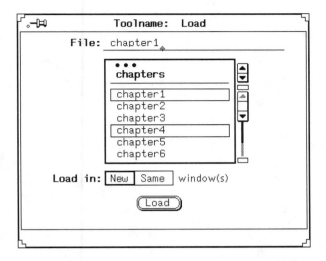

Figure 6-6   A Load command window with a nonexclusive hierarchical scrolling list.

The Browse Window Item

Choosing the Browse window item opens a file manager window to help users find the desired file to load. Consult the documentation for your toolkit for details about interclient communication and communicating with the file manager.

☑ Provide the Browse window item when you want to facilitate interaction between your application and the file manager.

The New Item

Choosing the New window item opens an additional window with an empty file without affecting any previously opened files.

☑ Provide the New window item on the File menu when you want users to be able to open a new window with an empty file.

The Print Menu Item

The Print Menu item provides you with a way to output data from your application to a printer.

The Print submenu should have at least the following items:

☐ File

☐ Selection

☐ Options . . .

Choosing the File item prints the file using existing settings. It is a good idea to provide users with this quick way to print from your application without displaying a command window. You can replace the word "File" with a term more appropriate for your application: "Document," "Database," or "Table," for example.

Choosing the Selection item prints the selection using existing settings.

You can add other, application-specific units between File and Selection. For example, a desktop publishing application might include items for "Chapter," "Section," or "Page." The order of the items should progress from the largest to the smallest unit, with Selection being the last item in the sequence, regardless of the size of the selection.

The Options window item opens a command window that permits users to set options for the printer.

☑ When defining printing options, consider providing parameters that accommodate both basic and more sophisticated printers, as well as providing settings that permit users to format and print the data from your application.

☑ When more than one printer is available to users, provide a way to switch between printers.

Figure 6-7 shows an example of a Print Options command window. The Always Displayed option automatically displays the Print Options command window whenever printing is initiated from a menu or from the keyboard.

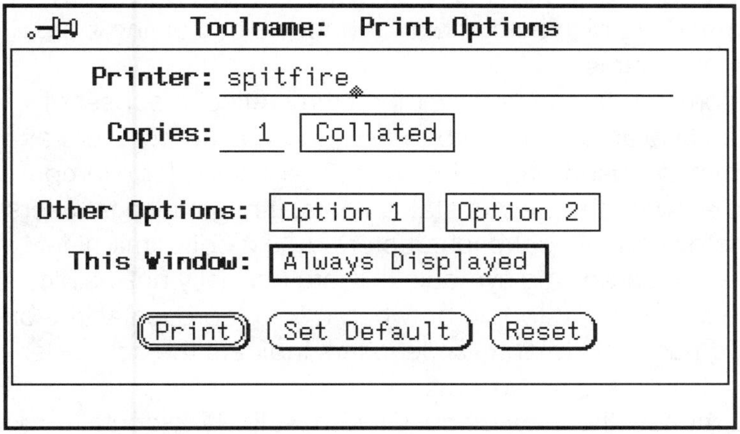

```
.—ᄆᄆ        Toolname:  Print Options

      Printer: spitfire▴

      Copies:   1  | Collated |


Other Options: | Option 1 |  | Option 2 |
  This Window: | Always Displayed |

       (Print) (Set Default) (Reset)
```

Figure 6-7   A Print Options command window.

☑ Provide Reset and Set Default buttons in the Print Options command
   window to allow users to configure the settings.

You can provide a nonexclusive hierarchical scrolling list as part of the Print
Options command window to allow users to be able to select and batch-print
a number of files.

☑ Consider including a way for users to batch-print files from your application from the Print Options command window.

The View Menu

The View menu provides users with controls that show alternative perspectives for data in your application. These can include visual differences to the data in the base window, such as guide rulers or formatting symbols. They can also include commands to display command windows containing status, information, or additional controls.

In some cases, the commands on the View menu may reflect a subset of commands that are also available from a property window, allowing users a shortcut access to commonly used properties. A 3270 emulator, for example, might use this menu to activate the view of status lights. It might also let users display or suppress the display of control characters. A text editor might let users control the display of paragraph symbols that are normally not visible. A file manager might use this menu to toggle between iconic representations of files and a text list of file names. It might also let users indicate the sort order or filtering of the list.

Of the four standard menus, the View menu is the most likely to contain controls that are specific to the type of data presented in your application.

☑ Use the View menu to offer functions that allow users to control how information is displayed.

A simplified View menu structure for a desktop publishing package is shown in Figure 6-8.

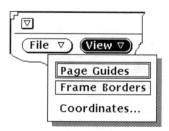

Figure 6-8   A typical View menu structure.

The Edit Menu

The Edit menu contains commands that allow users to enter, change, and delete the data displayed in the base window.

☑ Use the Edit menu to present standard controls that are related to editing objects.

☑ Always provide, as a minimum, Cut, Copy, Paste, Delete, and Undo functions from the Edit menu.

Users expect editing commands such as Cut/Copy/Paste to occur in a certain sequence.

☑ Be sure to present standard commands in the same order everywhere they occur.

For example, if you also include Cut/Copy/Paste commands on a pop-up Edit menu, be sure to present them in the same order on both menus.

☑ Use the following order and grouping for these commands on an edit menu:

- Select All
- Undo
- Again

- Cut
- Copy
- Paste

- Delete
- Clear All

☑ Always use the clipboard for Cut/Copy/Paste editing operations so that users can transfer data between applications.

☑ Do not provide application-only clipboards. If the clipboard provided by your OPEN LOOK toolkit cannot accommodate all of the formatting required by your application, then, as a minimum, provide basic vanilla data to the OPEN LOOK toolkit clipboard.

A typical Edit menu structure is shown in Figure 6-9.

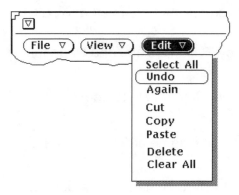

Figure 6-9   A typical Edit menu structure.

The Select All Command Item

☑ Provide a Select All command item on the Edit menu when it is useful to highlight all of the objects in the region that contains the input area.

☑ If your application has multiple areas between which users frequently switch, or if the parent area is difficult to select, change the Select All command to a menu item titled Select. Put two commands: All and Parent on the Select submenu. The default command is All.

Figure 6-10 shows an example of the Select submenu.

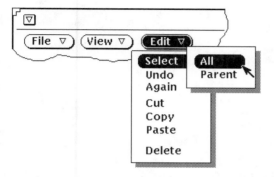

Figure 6-10   A Select submenu.

The All command selects everything. The Parent command highlights the region that contains the current selection. For example, if a circle is selected inside a larger rectangle, choosing Parent would highlight the rectangle. This feature is useful when objects that contain other objects have narrow, difficult-to-select borders. For instance, desktop publishing packages often deactivate the display of text frame borders. By using the Parent command, users can select a frame border without needing to display it.

Undo

The Undo command item reverses the previous action. Undo can have additional options. For example, it can provide items for multiple levels of undo. Alternatively, it can provide a choice between reversing the previous action or undoing all actions, as shown in Figure 6-11.

Figure 6-11   An Edit menu with enhanced functions.

☑   As a minimum, support at least one level of undo for your application.

Again

☑   Provide the Again command item on the Edit menu to allow users to repeat the last action.

Cut

☑   Provide the Cut command item on the Edit menu to allow users to remove the current selection and place it on the clipboard.

☑   Consider providing users with the ability to overwrite or append items to the clipboard by changing Cut to a menu item. Provide Overwrite and Append items on the Cut submenu.

Copy

☑   Provide the Copy command item on the Edit menu to allow users to place a copy of the current selection on the clipboard.

☑ Consider providing users with the ability to overwrite or append items to the clipboard by changing Copy to a menu item. Provide Overwrite and Append items on the Copy submenu.

Paste

☑ Provide the Paste command item on the Edit menu to allow users to insert the contents of the clipboard at the current insert point.

☑ When providing an Edit menu for lists, consider changing Paste to a menu item with Before and After items on the submenu to provide users with more flexibility in inserting items into the list.

Delete

☑ Provide the Delete command item on the Edit menu to allow users to remove the current selection without placing it on the clipboard.

Clear All

☑ Provide the Clear command item on the Edit menu to allow users to clear the contents of the insert area.

The Properties Menu Button

Properties are values that can be applied to the application itself or to selected objects within the application. A terminal emulator, for example, might have modem properties that are applied to the application as a whole.

☑ Always provide a property window that contains properties that can be applied to the application as a whole. If there are no user-settable

properties, display a property window with read-only information informing users that your application has no global properties for them to set.

To set properties within an application, users select one or more objects
and then display a property window. Many applications, however, also have
properties for objects that are not selectable or are not "intuitively" selectable.
A text editor, for example, might have style listings (pre-recorded properties
that can be applied to text). In these cases, there is no obvious selection for
users to make before pressing the Properties button on the keyboard or using
the Properties button in the control area.

☑   Consider making the categories of the application properties available
    from the Properties menu.

Properties that do not correspond to the selection belong in the application's Property window. Make the categories of the application's properties
available from the Properties menu. Figure 6-12 shows a typical Properties
menu. Selection, the default, opens the property window for the currently
selected object. The items after selection correspond to categories in the
application's Property window.

Figure 6-12   A typical Properties menu.

Adding to the Standard Button Menus

All of the standard control area menus can be tailored to the requirements of your application. When your application provides additional functions that relate to filing, include them on the File menu. Do the same for the View and Edit menus. These menus are most likely to vary from application to application.

Use items on each of the File, View, Edit, and Properties menus that make sense to users of your application. When an item does not make sense for your application, do not include it. You should also add items that provide functionality specific to your application.

For example, users expect certain commands (such as Cut, Copy, Paste, Again, and Undo) to be available on the Edit menu. Other, more specific, editing functions might also be appropriate for your application. In the example shown in Figure 6-13, the developer of a hypothetical spreadsheet application has supplemented the suggested Edit menu items. Paste and Delete have been changed into menu items that display submenus with additional choices, allowing users to specify which properties of the cell to Paste or Delete.

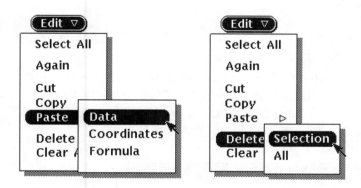

Figure 6-13 An Edit menu with customized submenus.

Adding to the Basic Control Area

☑ When appropriate, add specific, frequently used controls to the control area of your base window.

☑ If most of your users access a command most of the time they use the application, put it in the control area.

In addition to customizing the File, View, Edit, and Properties menus, you can put controls of any other type—buttons, settings, check boxes, text fields, sliders, and gauges—in the control area of your base window.

Probably the most common design is to augment the standard menu buttons with one or two other buttons for the most frequently performed operations, as shown in Figure 6-14.

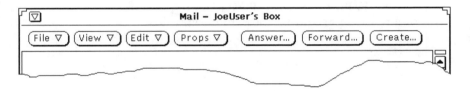

Figure 6-14 A control area with additional buttons.

Sometimes it is appropriate for you to put a frequently used text field in the control area of the base window, as shown in Figure 6-15. In this example, users can type text in the text field and click SELECT on the Find button to search for the specified text.

Figure 6-15 A control area with a text field.

208

When you are designing a complex application with many operations, the challenge is how best to organize all the features so that users can find a particular operation easily.

☑ One rule that goes a long way toward making a feature-rich application easy to use is to take an "intention-based" rather than an "object-based" approach.

An intention-based approach presents menu buttons in the control area that are organized around actions that users perform rather than objects that users manipulate. Figure 6-16 shows a design for an intention-based control area.

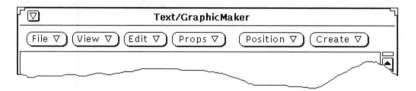

Figure 6-16 An intention-based application is easy to use.

Users would create an object of any type by choosing an item on the Create menu. A primary advantage of an intention-based control area, especially for applications that have objects of several types, is that the number of controls is reduced because each control can tailor its behavior to reflect the type of object selected. For example, selecting a circle and choosing Properties displays properties for circles. In this type of design, you do not need to provide a separate Circles menu button. Another advantage of the intention-based approach is that, although the objects (nouns) vary from application to application, the intentions (verbs) are more broadly applicable. You can use the same menu buttons consistently across a family of applications, leveraging off of existing applications.

An object-based design must, however, provide a different menu button for each type of object, as shown in Figure 6-17.

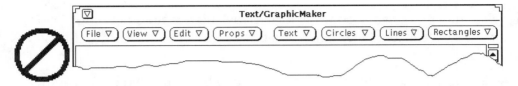

Figure 6-17 An object-based application requires too many basic controls.

Choosing Controls

The OPEN LOOK UI provides the following controls:

☐ Buttons and abbreviated buttons

☐ Items on menus

☐ Exclusive and nonexclusive settings

☐ Check boxes

☐ Text and numeric fields

☐ Sliders and gauges

☐ Scrolling lists

Read-only messages are also part of the OPEN LOOK UI controls. See Chapter 9 for information about application messages.

The following paragraphs provide guidelines for when to use a specific control and describe alternate controls for presenting the same information.

Buttons and Abbreviated Buttons

☑ Use command buttons to issue direct commands.

☑ Use window buttons (buttons with titles that are followed by ...) to open up additional windows.

☑ Use menu buttons to group related commands or settings together on a menu.

   Figure 6-18 shows an abbreviated menu button with the current choice to the right.

Speed: ▷ 1200 bps

Figure 6-18 An abbreviated menu button shows the current choice.

   Figure 6-19 shows the same abbreviated menu button with its menu displayed.

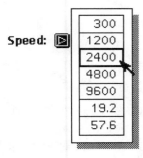

Figure 6-19 An abbreviated menu button and its menu.

Items on Menus

☑ Use command items to issue direct commands.

☑ Use window items to open up additional windows.

☑ Use menu items to group related commands or settings together on a submenu.

See Chapter 8 for more information about menus.

Exclusive Settings

☑ Use exclusive settings to present a group of choices when only one choice may be active at a time.

☑ Use exclusive settings when the number of choices is small, generally less than eight.

☑ When you need to present more choices than will fit comfortably in the available space, use an abbreviated menu button or a scrolling list.

Figure 6-20 shows an example of a exclusive setting.

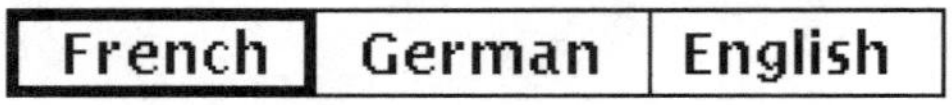

| French | German | English |

Figure 6-20 Exclusive settings are used when there is room for all the settings.

Sometimes it makes sense for users to be able to turn off all the choices in an exclusive setting. Your toolkit provides a succinct way to do this without adding any settings. This variation of exclusive settings permits users to click SELECT on a choice that is already on to turn it off, eliminating the need for the extra choice. Figure 6-21 shows an example with all the choices off, indicating that there is no current fill pattern.

Pattern:

Figure 6-21 A variation of an exclusive setting with no setting chosen.

Another way to accommodate this need is by adding a choice that means "none," as shown in Figure 6-22.

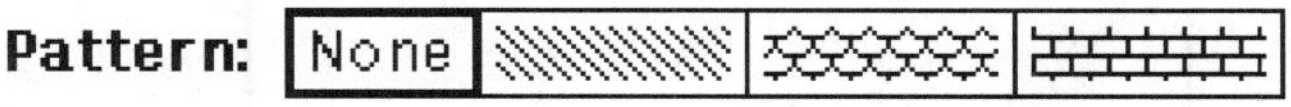

Pattern: | None | \\\\\\\\\\ | XXXXXX | ░░░░░░ |

Figure 6-22 Adding a choice that means "none" to an exclusive setting.

Nonexclusive Settings

☑ Use nonexclusive settings to present choices that are independent of one another.

It is quite common to group multiple nonexclusive settings opposite a single label, as shown in Figure 6-23.

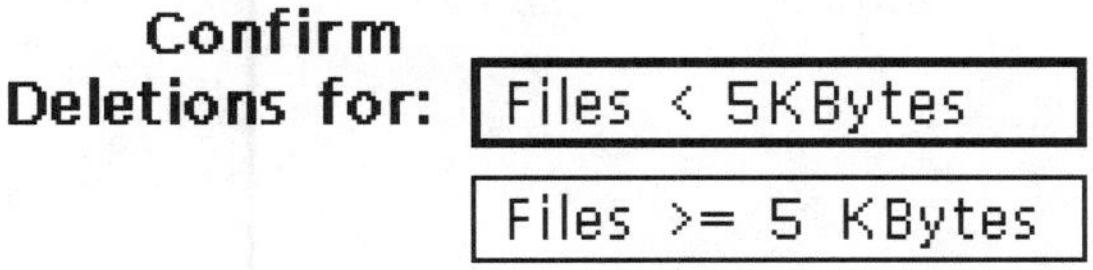

Confirm
Deletions for: | Files < 5KBytes |
| Files >= 5 KBytes |

Figure 6-23 Grouping multiple nonexclusive settings opposite a single label.

An alternate way to present choices that are independent of one another is by using check boxes, which are described in the following section.

Check Boxes

Check boxes can be used for a single control, but they are best used in groups. When arranged in a matrix, check boxes provide a compact way to allow users to set groups of related properties. In the example shown in Figure 6-24, users can set file permissions using check boxes.

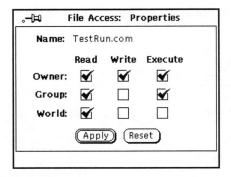

Figure 6-24 Check boxes arranged in a matrix.

☑ Use check boxes when a control has a yes/no or on/off state.

☑ Use check boxes for matrices when labels would otherwise have to be repeated.

As an alternative to check boxes, nonexclusive settings may be used.

Text and Numeric Fields

☑ Use text and/or numeric fields to let users type information.

Text and numeric fields can stand alone or be combined with exclusive settings, nonexclusive settings, buttons, sliders, and scrolling lists. Figure 6-25 shows some examples of text fields.

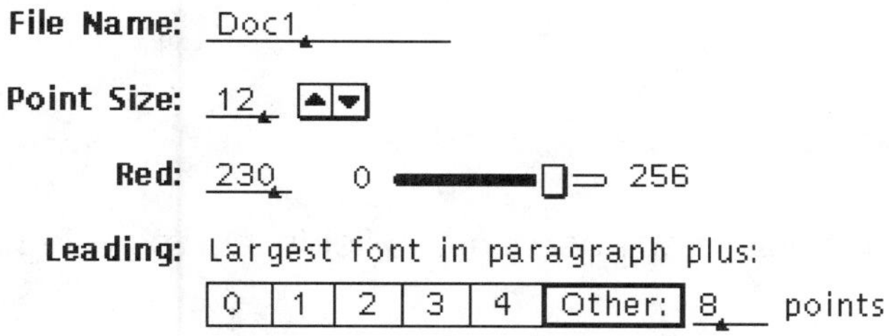

File Name: Doc1_____

Point Size: 12_ ▲▼

Red: 230_   0 ▬▬▬□⇒ 256

Leading: Largest font in paragraph plus:

| 0 | 1 | 2 | 3 | 4 | Other: | 8_ | points |

Figure 6-25 Some examples of text fields.

☑ Provide minimum and maximum values for numeric fields.

☑ Inactivate the arrow of the increment button when the maximum value is displayed. Inactivate the arrow of the decrement button when the minimum value is displayed.

☑ Use a numeric field when the range of numbers is discrete and exact values are required.

As an alternative to numeric fields, sliders, exclusive settings, and scrolling lists may be used.

Sliders

☑ Use sliders when users can set a range of values for an object, when there is a large range of values, and when accuracy is less important than relative position.

Figure 6-26 shows a basic horizontal slider. The variations and enhancements provided for sliders depends on your toolkit. See Chapter 7 for more information about labeling and formatting sliders.

Red: 0 ━━━━━□⇒ 256

Figure 6-26   A basic horizontal slider.

As an alternative to sliders, exclusive settings, numeric fields, and scrolling lists may be used.

Gauges

☑ Use gauges to display status information, such as percentage of disk usage, or to track the progress of a lengthy operation.

Figure 6-27 shows a typical gauge.

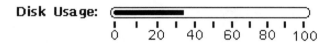

Figure 6-27   A typical gauge.

Scrolling Lists

☑ Use scrolling lists to present an unbounded list of items in a small, well-defined region and to present lists that users can customize by editing.

☑ Make the scrolling list editable when users can change the items or rearrange the order in which the items are displayed.

Scrolling lists are by far the most flexible type of OPEN LOOK UI control. Unlike nonexclusive and exclusive settings, a scrolling list can have chosen items that are not visible because the items can be scrolled out of view.

☑ Use an exclusive scrolling list in lieu of an exclusive setting when there are too many choices to fit in the available space, when the number of choices varies as the application runs, or when you want users to be able to edit the list.

Figure 6-28 presents fonts in an exclusive scrolling list.

Figure 6-28 A nonexclusive scrolling list of fonts.

☑ Use a nonexclusive scrolling list in place of nonexclusive settings when the number of choices is very large or varies dynamically.

Figure 6-29 shows a scrolling list with choices that are added and removed while the application runs.

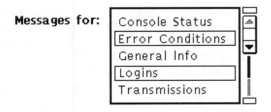

Figure 6-29 A nonexclusive scrolling list that changes as the application runs.

In the example shown in Figure 6-30, the nonexclusive scrolling list contains a large number of choices.

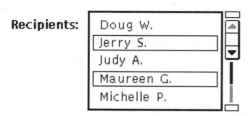

Figure 6-30 A nonexclusive scrolling list with a large number of items.

☑ Use a hierarchical scrolling list when the items can be grouped into categories.

For example, projects might be divided into a container for each month of the year. By default, each container is represented by a bullet to the left of its name. If the container represents a real-world object, such as a folder, substitute a glyph of that object in place of the bullet. Figure 6-31 shows an example of a hierarchical scrolling list for a company directory.

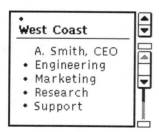

Figure 6-31 A hierarchical scrolling list.

Scrolling List Menus

The OPEN LOOK UI specifies a basic set of menus for scrolling lists.

☑ Add application-specific functionality to the basic and editable Scrolling List menus when appropriate. When a scrolling list menu contains commands that are available elsewhere in your application, display them in the same order as is used in their other occurrences.

Figure 6-32 shows the menu for a scrolling list of exclusive items. The arrow shows the suggested place to add items to the exclusive Scrolling List menu.

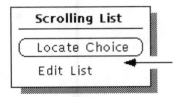

Figure 6-32 The arrow shows the suggested place to add items to the exclusive Scrolling List menu.

Figure 6-33 shows the menu for a scrolling list of nonexclusive items. The arrow shows the suggested place to add items to the nonexclusive Scrolling List menu.

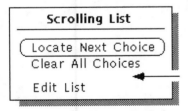

Figure 6-33 The arrow shows the suggested place to add items to the nonexclusive Scrolling List menu.

When users are editing the scrolling list, the items on the Scrolling List menu change to provide editing functions.

You can add items to the Scrolling List menu. For example, you can include items normally found in the Edit menu. If you provide Cut, Copy, and Paste commands, use them in that order. Figure 6-34 shows the editing menu for a scrolling list that has no additional data beyond that which is displayed in the list. Choosing Change or Insert from this menu displays lines for text entry within the scrolling list. The arrow shows the suggested place to add items to this menu.

Figure 6-34 The arrow shows the suggested place to add items to the editing Scrolling List menu.

Figure 6-35 shows the default Edit menu for a scrolling list with items that have additional data beyond what is displayed in the scrolling list. Choosing the Properties or Insert item on this menu displays a property window. The arrow shows the suggested place to add items to this menu.

Figure 6-35   The arrow shows the suggested place to add items to the editing Scrolling List menu.

Summary of When to Use OPEN LOOK UI Controls

Table 6-1 lists typical application functions and suggests appropriate OPEN LOOK UI controls that you can use.

Table 6-1 Summary of OPEN LOOK UI control functionality and usage

Functionality	OPEN LOOK UI Control
Issue a command	Command button Abbreviated command button Command item Item in a scrolling list
Open a window	Window button Abbreviated window button Window item
Display a menu	Menu button Abbreviated menu button Menu item
Set the state of an object	Exclusive setting Nonexclusive setting Check box Slider Item in a scrolling list
Set one of a range of values	Exclusive setting Slider Text field Numeric field
Enter data	Text field Numeric field Slider Nonscrollable text region Scrollable text region
Show status information	Gauge Read-only message

Feedback for OPEN LOOK UI Controls

Interaction is a two-way street. It is just as important for your application to let users know what's going on as it is for users to tell your application what to do. Users expect consistent feedback so that they understand what is happening. This section describes the various kinds of feedback for OPEN LOOK UI controls. The OPEN LOOK toolkit provides the standard visual feedback for each kind of control to communicate clearly to users each time they activate a command. As an example, look at the following visual changes that occur when users activate a command button.

Normal Feedback

A typical command button has a label with a border, as shown in Figure 6-36.

Figure 6-36 A typical command button.

Highlighting Feedback

To activate the button, users move the pointer onto the button and press the SELECT mouse button. The button highlights to give users feedback that the command button has been pushed, as shown in Figure 6-37.

Press SELECT

Figure 6-37 A highlighted command button.

At this time, users can decide whether or not to complete the action. Moving the pointer off the button and releasing SELECT removes the highlighting from the button, but does not activate the command. To activate the command, users release SELECT while the button is highlighted. The highlighting of controls is provided as part of your OPEN LOOK toolkit.

Busy Feedback

While the control is being executed, the button displays a light gray pattern that is the standard busy pattern, as shown in Figure 6-38.

Release SELECT

Figure 6-38 A busy command button.

Some commands may execute quickly; others may take longer to perform.

☑ When the application as a whole cannot accept input, the header should also display the standard busy pattern.

When the action is complete, the button returns to its usual appearance, as shown in Figure 6-39.

Action complete

Figure 6-39 A command button after the action has been completed.

Buttons and menu items are the only controls that use the busy pattern.
When users initiate an operation such as saving a file, the application typically does not respond to further input until the operation is completed. When the application as a whole cannot respond to input, the button displays the standard busy pattern. In addition, the window is considered busy, and its header displays the standard busy pattern. Users can work in another window and tell at a glance when the busy window is ready for input. Figure 6-40 shows a window that is busy saving a file.

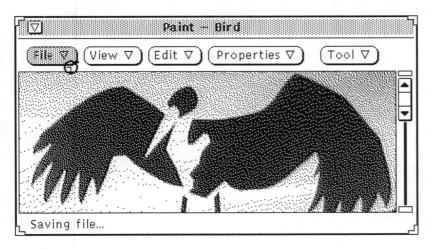

Figure 6-40 Busy window feedback.

Note that the File menu button shows the same busy feedback, indicating which operation is in progress, and the busy pointer is displayed when it is in the busy window.

A busy icon displays the standard busy pattern in its background area, as shown in Figure 6-41.

Figure 6-41   Busy icon feedback.

Inactive Controls

It is common for controls that operate on the selection to be *inactive* when there is no selection or when the action cannot be performed. For example, controls are typically inactive in the following circumstances:

☐ In a word processing program, the Cut and Copy commands in the Edit menu are inactive when no text is selected.

☐ When there is nothing on the clipboard, the Paste command in the Edit menu is inactive.

☐ On a scrollbar, the top arrow is dimmed when the scrollbar cable is at the top of the pane, showing users that the contents of the pane cannot be scrolled any farther in that direction.

In the OPEN LOOK UI, inactive controls are *dimmed*, as shown in Figure 6-42.

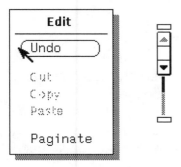

Figure 6-42 Inactive controls are dimmed.

Inactive controls have several advantages. Sometimes showing an inactive control helps users interpret the controls that are active, as shown in the example in Figure 6-43.

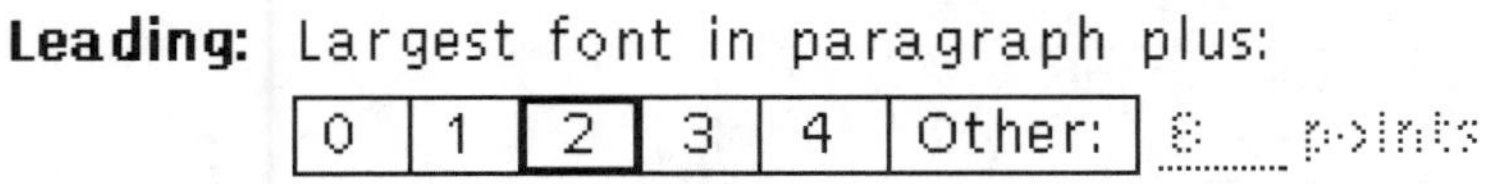

Leading: Largest font in paragraph plus:

| 0 | 1 | 2 | 3 | 4 | Other: | 8____ points |

Figure 6-43 An inactive control helps users interpret the information.

Alternatively, you could choose to hide the text field and units that are shown as inactive in Figure 6-43 when Other is not chosen.

☑ Whether you make controls inactive or hide them, be sure to be consistent throughout your application.

Inactive controls minimize changes to the appearance of a window. Showing and hiding controls can be distracting, particularly if the controls come and go frequently.

☑ Hide controls that are used infrequently. Dim frequently used controls when they are inactive.

Indeterminate Feedback

Settings are used to change the attributes of a command or those of a selected object. They also reflect the state of the selected object. When more than one object is selected, and/or for some other reason more than one value exists for a single setting, the setting provides *indeterminate feedback* to show that the setting does not accurately reflect the current state of the selected object. Indeterminate feedback is similar to inactive feedback, but only the borders of the indeterminate settings are dimmed; the labels themselves are not dimmed. Figure 6-44 shows a property window with indeterminate settings.

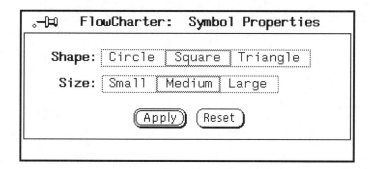

Figure 6-44 Indeterminate settings have dimmed borders.

In this example, users selected multiple objects and then displayed the property window. The Square and Medium settings appear to be chosen, though the setting borders are dimmed. Indeterminate settings reflect the condition of the first selected object. The definition of the first object varies based on the type of object that is selected. In the case of text selection, for example, the first object is the first character in the highlighted selection. In the case of graphics, the first object is the first object users selected.

☑ Use indeterminate feedback whenever the selection reflects more than one value and the setting can show only one value at a time.

Change Bars

A Level 2 toolkit provides *change bars* for text fields and for all controls in property windows. A change bar is a small vertical bar that is displayed to the left of the label of a property whose value has been changed but whose new value has not yet been applied. Users can see the visual cue provided by the change bars and review the property window changes before applying them. Figure 6-45 shows a property window with a single change bar.

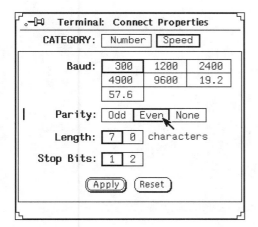

Figure 6-45 Change bars mark settings that have been changed but not applied.

Dimmed Change Bars

You may want to restrict input for a text or numeric field to a set of legal values.

☑ When you restrict input to a set of legal values, you need to validate the input once users have finished entering it.

☑ You can show unvalidated input by displaying a dimmed change bar, as shown in Figure 6-46.

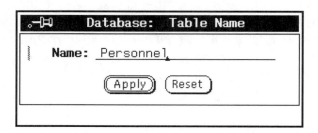

Figure 6-46 Dimmed change bars show unvalidated input.

☑ Display the dimmed bar as soon as users type a character.

☑ If the text field is displayed in a property window, change the bar to black after the contents of the field have been validated.

☑ If possible, validate the field immediately after users enter the value or change the setting.

☑ Alternatively, perform the validation when users apply the properties.

Validating when properties are applied is useful, especially when the property window requires a complete set of values before it can perform an action—for example, when a data communications application establishes a connection with a remote device. In the example shown in Figure 6-46, the input cannot be validated until the application tries to update the database server. If the database is local, the application can validate the field immediately.

See Chapter 9 for information about error messages for invalid input.

Default Controls for Menus and Pop-up Windows

To provide for efficient operation and shortcuts, each OPEN LOOK UI menu, without exception, must have a single default item. Users can change the default item at any time while using the application.

☑ Specify the initial default for each menu in your application.

☑ Make the default the most commonly used item on the menu.

If you do not specify a default for a particular menu, the toolkit makes the first item in the menu (which is the pushpin, if one is present) the default. Figure 6-47 shows an example of a Text menu with Undo as the default item.

Figure 6-47 A menu with a default item.

Users cannot change the default button for pop-up windows. Specifying a default button for each pop-up window permits users to activate the default using the Default Action keyboard accelerator. The OPEN LOOK UI specifies buttons for property windows and designates that Apply is the default.

☑ You must specify a default button for each pop-up window that has button controls.

Figure 6-48 shows an example of a pop-up window in which Search Forward is the default button.

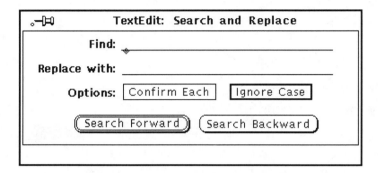

Figure 6-48 A command window with a default button.

Summary of Controls Feedback

Table 6-2 provides a summary of the kinds of feedback for each control.

Table 6-2   Summary of feedback for OPEN LOOK UI controls.

Control	Inactive	Indeter-minate	Busy	Default	Change Bars
Abbreviated menu	☐	☐	✓	☐	☐
Check boxes	✓	✓	☐	☐	✓
Command button	✓	☐	✓	✓	☐
Command item	✓	☐	✓	✓	☐
Gauges	✓	✓	☐	☐	☐
Menu button	☐	☐	✓	☐	☐
Menu item	☐	☐	✓	✓	☐
Settings	✓	✓	☐	✓	✓
Sliders	✓	✓	☐	☐	✓
Text Fields	✓	✓	☐	☐	✓
Window button	☐	☐	✓	☐	☐
Window item	☐	☐	✓	✓	☐

7

NAMING AND GROUPING CONTROLS

When an architect has designed the shape and number of rooms in a house, an interior designer determines what furniture to put in each room and chooses the fabric and texture for each item. Just as an interior designer wants the furnishings to blend harmoniously to create an environment for comfortable living, so you want to make the names of your controls easy to understand and intuitive to use. Pay careful attention to the names that you give to the controls in your application. Users appreciate clearly labeled and identifiable controls. The more obvious the label on a control is to users, the more they will feel that your application is easy to use.

This chapter provides guidelines for:

☐ How to name windows, icons, and controls

☐ How to label groups of controls

☐ How to group controls into larger categories

Titles

The following OPEN LOOK Graphical User Interface elements must have a unique *title* that identifies them to users. A button control, item, or setting can have a picture—called a *glyph*—as a title.

☐ Windows and icons
☐ Pop-up menus
☐ Button controls
☐ Items on menus
☐ Settings

Titles for Windows

The title you choose for the base window affects design elements in many other places in your application. It is used as a prefix for each command, property, and help window, and may be used as a title for the icon.

☑ Carefully consider how the title you choose for your base window works when it is used in icons and pop-up windows.

☑ Begin the title of each pop-up window with the application title followed by a colon, then the title of the pop-up window.

For example, a property window that displays paragraph properties for a text-editing application called OpenEdit would be named: OpenEdit: Paragraph Properties.

☑ If the name of the pop-up window is too long, drop the application title; but remember that without the title users might have difficulty telling which pop-up windows belong with the originating base window.

☑ Follow the application name for each command window with the same title that is on the window button or window item users choose to display the window.

☑ Follow the application name for each property window, as a minimum, with the title "Properties" and the name of the object it affects.

Each window title has the following characteristics, which are provided by your toolkit:

☐ It is displayed in a bold font in a font size appropriate for the scale of the window.

☐ It is centered in the header.

You are responsible for specifying the title, the punctuation, and the capitalization for each title of your application.

☑ Use initial capital letters for each word of the title (in languages that support capitalization).

Titles for Icons

Icons typically have both a glyph and a title, as shown in Figure 7-1.

Figure 7-1   An icon typically has both a glyph area and a text label.

When designing icon glyphs and titles, you first need to consider the overall size of the icon. The OPEN LOOK UI specifies a standard size for icons of 65 points square. Design both the image and the label of icons to fit within that size, if possible.

Occasionally, however, it makes sense for an application to deviate from the standard icon size. For example, it is common to use an icon to display a monthly calendar in its smallest form, as shown in Figure 7-2.

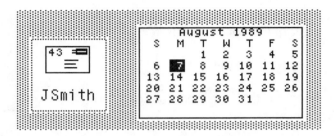

Figure 7-2   A standard icon (left) and a nonstandard icon (right).

Even using the smallest possible print, such an icon will be larger than the standard 65 points square.

The OPEN LOOK UI specifies a grid on the workspace for aligning icons. By default, that grid is 13 points square. The number 13 was chosen to allow the 65-point icons to be placed next to one another. In Level 2 toolkits, users can define a different grid spacing or turn the grid off.

☑ Keep the workspace grid in mind when designing an icon of nonstandard size. Make the icon a number divisible by 13, as required by the OPEN LOOK UI.

Nonstandard icons with dimensions such as 52 by 65, 65 by 101, and so on (all numbers divisible by 13), will fit neatly on the workspace grid.

☑ Make the icon for your application easily identifiable. One obvious way to make it identifiable is to use the title of the icon as the title for your base window, as suggested earlier.

Figure 7-3 shows an example of an icon title that is the same as the application title.

Figure 7-3   An icon that uses the application title.

☑ When your application opens a new base window for each document or file, use the name of the document as the icon title, and use the icon glyph to show that the documents are related to the application icon.

☑ Use the image in the icon as a visual signature for your application and as the text label for the document created by the application.

Figure 7-4 shows icons for an application with a primary base window and a set of documents. The Convert icon on the left represents the conversion application. The icons on the right represent data files produced by the conversion application; they use a slightly modified version of the glyph from the Convert icon.

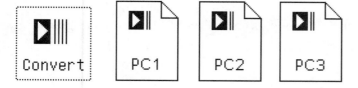

Figure 7-4   An application that has separate icons for individual documents.

☑ If your application uses multiple base windows, be sure that the icon for each base window has a unique label that indicates its function.

In the example shown in Figure 7-5, a mail application has an in-box icon and a composition window icon.

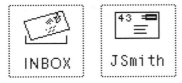

Figure 7-5   Icons for an application with multiple base windows.

☑ Strive for a balance of dark and light in designing your icon glyph.

☑ Keep the glyphs in icons simple.

The glyph design for your icons is a part of your overall presentation. Icons that are too solidly dark tend to be overpowering and distracting, and those that are too white can easily become lost in a crowded workspace.

Figure 7-6 shows examples of dark, light, and balanced icon designs.

Figure 7-6   Too dark (left), too light (middle), and balanced (right) icon designs.

Attempts to render a faithful picture in the small image area of an icon can end up looking too busy. Figure 7-7 shows examples of sparse, detailed, and balanced icon glyphs.

Figure 7-7   Too sparse (left), too busy (middle), and balanced (right) icon designs.

☑   When appropriate, use icons to show a change in the state of your application.

You can use the icon to provide feedback to users from the application when the base window is closed. A good example of showing a change of state is a mail application that changes the design of the glyph when new mail has arrived, as shown in Figure 7-8.

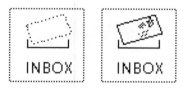

Figure 7-8   Icon glyphs can show a change of state in the application.

Titles for Pop-up Menus

Each pop-up menu must have a title. The title helps users, particularly new ones, identify the menu. For example, when you group frequently used editing commands on a pop-up menu, title the pop-up menu "Edit."

☑ Choose titles for pop-up menus with care so that they are meaningful based on the object selected or the region under the pointer. Keep them short to minimize the width of the menu.

☑ Do not use the word "menu" as part of the title.

Figure 7-9 shows the Workspace pop-up menu.

Figure 7-9 The Workspace menu is an example of a pop-up menu with an appropriate title.

Titles for Buttons

Buttons provide three functions to users of your application:

☐ Executing a command

☐ Displaying a menu

☐ Displaying a pop-up window

Each of these functions has a distinct visual design element or *symbol* so that users know what action to expect when they choose a button.
You specify the following characteristics for each button in your application:

☐ A glyph or text title in the regular font

☐ Initial capital letters (in languages that support capitalization)

☐ Centering in the border when buttons are arranged horizontally

☐ Left-justification when buttons are arranged vertically

☐ The width of the button, if not automatically defined by your toolkit

☑ Always use the OPEN LOOK UI symbols that show which controls are used to display windows (...) and which controls are used to display menus (an open triangle).

Users quickly learn that a button or item with a *menu mark* (a hollow triangle pointing either downward or to the right), is used to display menus, and that a button or item that is followed by a *window mark* (three dots) is used to display a window.

☑ Use unique single-word titles as much as possible.

Single-word titles are easier to scan and keep the size of the controls to a minimum. Titles should be as brief as possible while still conveying to users the information that they need.

Command Buttons

A button that executes a command is called a *command button* and has a unique title or glyph identifying the function that it performs.

Figure 7-10 shows an example of a command button with text and an example of one with a glyph title.

Figure 7-10 Buttons with text and glyph titles.

Menu Buttons

A button that displays a menu is called a *menu button* and always has a menu mark symbol following the title or glyph. The menu mark is a hollow triangle pointing either downward or to the right. The direction in which the menu mark points shows users where the menu is displayed when they press the MENU mouse button.

Figure 7-11 shows an example of horizontal and vertical menu buttons, with the Edit menu displayed.

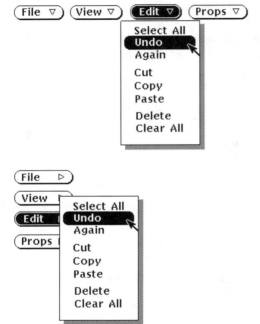

Figure 7-11 Menu buttons always have a menu mark symbol showing where the menu is displayed (either below or to the left of the menu button).

☑ Left-justify button titles and use a right-facing menu mark when menu buttons are arranged vertically.

☑ Center button titles and use a downward-facing menu mark when menu buttons are arranged horizontally.

These formatting arrangements may be handled automatically by your toolkit.

☑ Always label menu buttons with the type of command or option that their menus contain. Never give a menu button the same label as one of the controls in its menu.

The toolkit provides the menu mark when you specify a menu button.

Window Buttons

A button that displays a window is called a *window button* and always has a window mark symbol following the title or the glyph. Use the window mark on any button that displays a window, whether it is a base window or a pop-up window.

Figure 7-12 shows a window button with its window mark.

(Addressee...)

Figure 7-12 A window button always has a window mark following the title.

☑ Define the title for each window button and follow it with a window mark. Depending on the toolkit, the window mark may be provided automatically. If it is not provided by the toolkit, provide it as part of the text string for the button title.

Glyphs or Titles

Just because the OPEN LOOK UI is a "graphical" user interface does not mean that you should overload your application with glyphs. Pictures are fun for both the designer and users, and it is tempting to overuse them. Unless each function has a glyph that is easily identifiable—especially to a beginning user—glyphs can make your application appear obscure and inapproachable.

There are several reasons for using simple text titles instead of glyphs, especially for buttons that are displayed in the control area of the base window:

□ The control area, as part of the background of your application, does not need to be packed full of visual excitement. Although such a control area might be interesting at first, it becomes tiring with repeated use. Too much visual activity tends to distract users from the job at hand and makes your application more difficult to use.

□ Buttons with glyphs tend to be larger than buttons with text titles. Minimizing the size of buttons gives users more room on the workspace to perform the real functions of data manipulation.

□ Usually it is difficult to find an appropriate, easy-to-identify picture for each button. You may have one or two really good glyphs that clearly represent the function to be performed, and you may have to make up other, less well-defined glyphs to complete the set.

☑ Use restraint in visual design.

Figure 7-13 shows buttons with glyphs. Can you guess what each of these buttons does?

Figure 7-13 Buttons with glyph titles.

☑ Avoid using buttons with glyphs in the control area of your base window.

One way to solve this problem is to put text titles underneath the glyphs, as shown in Figure 7-14. However, adding titles to these buttons makes them even busier and might increase the height of the buttons.

☑ Do not combine glyphs and titles within the border of the same button. If the button needs a title, then the glyphs are unclear.

Figure 7-14 Buttons with glyph and text titles.

Figure 7-15 shows the same set of buttons with text titles. These buttons are easy for users to understand.

☑ Use short, easy-to-scan text titles for buttons in the control area of your base window.

Figure 7-15 Buttons with clear, short titles.

Follow these guidelines for deciding when to use glyphs as button titles:

☑ Use glyphs when they represent well-known symbols or conventions and their meaning is clear.

☑ Use glyphs when they represent widely-used industry conventions.

Figure 7-16 shows an example of a control area with buttons that represent industry conventions. The word "Insert" is placed to the left of the flowcharting buttons to make their purpose clear. The label is not required and can be omitted when the use of the buttons is straightforward.

☑ Do not overload your application with glyphs.

A one-word title can sometimes clearly identify a control when a glyph might confuse users.

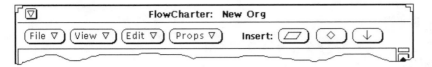

Figure 7-16 A control area with glyph titles that represent standard flowcharting symbols.

Titles for Items on Menus

Menu items provide the same functionality and operational feedback as button controls but have a slightly different look. Menu items provide the same three functions that button controls provide to users of your application: executing a command, displaying a menu, or displaying a window.

☑ When naming items or settings on a menu, make the first word of each title unique.

Users can view the default settings for menus without displaying the menu. If items have duplicate information at the beginning of the title, viewing of default items is much less useful.

Command Items

An item that executes a command is called a command item and has a unique title or glyph identifying the function that it performs.

Figure 7-17 shows examples of menus with text and glyph command items.

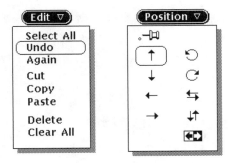

Figure 7-17   Menus with text and glyph command items.

☑   Decide on the title (either text or glyph) for each command item. Do not mix text and glyph items in the same menu.

Menu Items

An item that displays a submenu is called a menu item and always has a menu mark following the title or glyph. The menu mark is a hollow triangle pointing to the right to show users that the submenu is displayed to the right.

☑   Use menu items to display submenus containing groups of related commands.

☑   Decide on the title for each menu item. Submenus are always displayed to the right; therefore, the menu mark always points to the right.

Your toolkit automatically aligns the menu marks, right-justifying them.

Window Items

An item that displays a window is called a window item and always has a window mark following the title or the glyph.

☑ Use the window mark on any item that displays a window, whether it is a base window or a pop-up window.

☑ Decide on the title for each window item.

☑ Determine whether or not your toolkit provides the window mark. If it does not, include it as part of the text string of the window item.

The menu shown in Figure 7-18 has all three items: The Load and Save window items display pop-up windows, the New command item creates a new file, and the Print menu item displays a submenu with additional choices.

Figure 7-18 A menu with command, window, and menu items.

Titles for Settings

Each individual setting, whether exclusive or nonexclusive, has a title that is displayed inside the border for the setting. Settings are also grouped together and identified by a *label*. This section describes naming individual settings. See "Labels for Controls" later in this chapter for more information about labeling groups of settings.

☑ Define the title (either text or glyph) for each individual setting. Do not mix text and glyph settings within the same group.

☑ Left-justify setting titles when they are arranged vertically.

☑ Center setting titles when they are arranged horizontally.

☑ When arranging settings in a grid, keep each column of settings the same width.

Figure 7-19 shows some examples of setting titles and arrangements.

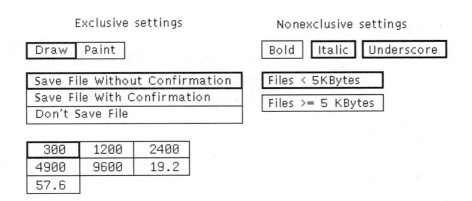

Figure 7-19   Some examples of exclusive and nonexclusive setting titles and arrangements.

Labels for Controls

A *label* is a text string that identifies a control that does not have an internal title or that identifies groups of related controls. The following OPEN LOOK UI controls do not have titles as an integral part of the control element, and therefore have labels:

☐ Text and numeric fields

☐ Abbreviated menu buttons

☐ Check boxes

☐ Sliders

☐ Gauges

☐ Scrolling lists

The following OPEN LOOK UI controls have titles, but fall naturally into groups that typically have a label.

☐ Exclusive settings

☐ Nonexclusive settings

Labels for these controls have the following characteristics:

☐ A text label followed by a colon positioned at the left of the control

☐ Bold font in a size appropriate for the scale of the window

☐ Initial capital letters (in languages that support capitalization)

☑ Specify an identifying label for each control or group of controls when needed.

☑ Use initial capital letters (in languages that support capitalization).

☑ Follow each label with a colon.

☑ When grouping labeled controls, right-justify the labels and align them by the colons.

Use the following guidelines for labeling controls:

☑ Use labels for controls that do not have titles, or for groups of controls.

☑ Always label controls in property or command windows.

☑ Do not label controls in a control area when the meaning is clear. Label controls in the control area when needed to avoid ambiguity.

☑ Keep labels short to make them easy to read at a glance.

☑ When the label is more than half the length of the group of controls, divide it into two lines.

☑ When the label has more than one line, horizontally align the baseline of the last line of the label with the baseline of text inside the first control.

Labeling Text Fields

Text fields allow users to enter text or numeric input. They can be single-line text fields or multilined boxed regions that may or may not have a scrollbar. Single-line text fields contain a built-in scrolling capability so that they can accommodate more characters than will fit in the visible length of the field.

☑ Specify both the visible length of the field and the maximum number of characters that the field can hold.

☑ Make the visible field long enough to accommodate a typical string without scrolling.

For example, if you expect users to type in a 24-character product name, do not make the field shorter than that unless there is a compelling reason to do so.

There are two equally acceptable approaches to labeling fields.

☑ Precede the field with a general label and follow it with a read-only message that specifies the unit.

This style is particularly useful when there are two related fields that can be grouped next to the same label, as shown in Figure 7-20.

Weight: 12   pounds 2   ounces

Figure 7-20 Two text fields with the same label, followed by a unit.

☑ Use the name of the unit as the label.

Figure 7-21 shows an example of a text field with the unit as the label.

Pounds: 12

Figure 7-21 A text field preceded by a unit as the label.

Labeling Abbreviated Menu Buttons

The abbreviated menu button typically has a label to the left and displays the current choice from the menu as read-only text to the right of the abbreviated button, as shown in Figure 7-22.

Speed: ▷ 1200 bps

Figure 7-22 An abbreviated menu button with a label on the left and the current choice on the right.

Users can display the button menu to see the full list of choices, as shown in Figure 7-23.

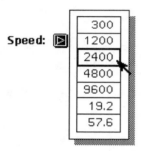

Figure 7-23 An abbreviated menu button with its menu displayed.

☑ Specify a label for the abbreviated menu button that describes the group of choices on the menu.

☑ Decide whether the menu is displayed below or to the right of the abbreviated menu button. Position the menu to the right in property and command windows. Position the menu below the abbreviated menu button in control areas.

Labeling Check Boxes

You can use check boxes for a single control, but they are best used in groups. When arranged in a matrix, check boxes provide a compact way to allow users to set groups of related properties.

Figure 7-24 shows check boxes arranged in a matrix.

	Read	Write	Execute
Owner:	☑	☑	☑
Group:	☑	☐	☑
World:	☑	☐	☐

Figure 7-24 Label rows and columns of a check box grid.

☑ When check boxes are presented in a matrix, provide a read-only message in bold at the top of each column and an appropriate label at the left.

Labeling Sliders

OPEN LOOK UI sliders provide you with a variety of labeling and formatting options. The options that are available to you depend on the toolkit you are using. The information presented in this section describes Level 2 toolkit variations and how to use them. If your toolkit does not provide these variations, you can construct them on your own by combining the slider with other OPEN LOOK UI controls.

☑ Provide a label when the slider settings are not obvious or intuitive.

You can provide the following variations to sliders:

☐ End point labels to show users the minimum or maximum value for the slider
☐ Current value labels to show users where the slider is set on the scale of possible values

□ End boxes to allow users to set the slider quickly to either its minimum or its maximum value

□ Tick marks to show a range of possible values

End-point Labels

☑ Provide end-point labels to show users the minimum and maximum values that can be set with a slider.

Figure 7-25 shows an example of a basic slider with a category label and end-point labels.

Red: 0 ▬▬▬■□⇒ 256

Figure 7-25 End-point labels for a slider show minimum and maximum values.

The end-point labels need not be numeric. Figure 7-26 shows an example of a slider with nonnumeric labels.

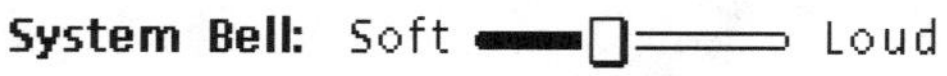

System Bell: Soft ▬■□══════ Loud

Figure 7-26 A slider with nonnumeric end-point labels.

Current Value

You can show the current value for the slider either as a read-only message (top) or as a text field (bottom), as shown in Figure 7-27.

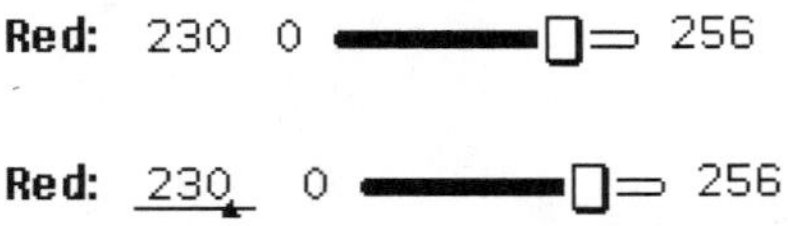

Red: 230 0 ━━━━■◻⇒ 256

Red: 230 0 ━━━━■◻⇒ 256

Figure 7-27 Sliders with current value fields.

☑ When you provide numeric end points, include a current value field to show users the precise current value for the slider.

☑ Put the current value immediately following the label.

End Boxes

You can specify that the slider include *end boxes* that act as buttons and cause the drag box to jump directly to the minimum or maximum value when users click SELECT on an end box. Figure 7-28 shows a slider with end boxes.

Red: 230 0 ◻━━━━■◻⇒◻ 256

Figure 7-28 A slider with end boxes.

☑ Use end boxes only if you expect users to set the slider to its minimum or maximum setting frequently.

End boxes are not essential, and they make the slider more complex.

Tick Marks

Tick marks are small vertical lines that divide a slider into segments. You can enhance sliders with tick marks, as shown in Figure 7-29.

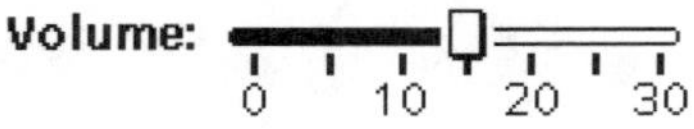

Volume:

Figure 7-29 A slider with tick marks and intermediate labels.

☑ Use tick marks as a visual embellishment, possibly accompanied by numeric labels that show specific intermediate values.

You can provide tick marks with an operational as well as a visual function. Specify that tick marks are active so that the drag box jumps to the nearest tick mark when users release SELECT.

☑ Use active tick marks when the slider has a fixed number of possible values.

Figure 7-30 shows one of the advantages of sliders. The slider has only six discrete positions. You might think that an exclusive setting would be a more straightforward way to present the options, but an exclusive setting requires a distinct label for each choice. Instead of having a series of labels such as Tiny, Small, Medium, Large, Extra Large, and Huge, the slider provides a more tasteful solution.

Size: Small ▬▬▢═══► Large

Figure 7-30 A slider with active tick marks.

Vertical Sliders

Sometimes it is more natural to display sliders vertically. Thermometers are a good example, because people often think of temperature ranging from low to high. Figure 7-31 shows an example of a vertical slider.

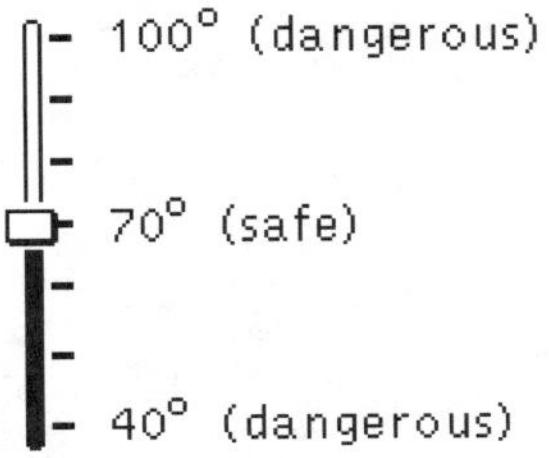

```
|- 100° (dangerous)
|-
|-
□- 70° (safe)
|-
|-
|- 40° (dangerous)
```

Figure 7-31 A vertical slider

☑ Use vertical sliders when the vertical orientation is more natural or when the object being represented has a vertical orientation.

☑ Use vertical sliders when the tick mark labels are lengthy.

Labeling Scrolling Lists

Scrolling lists can be displayed in command, property, and base windows. When the scrolling list is the only control in a window, the title of the window acts as the label for the scrolling list. When scrolling lists are combined with other controls, or when the function of the scrolling list may not be obvious from the contents of the list, provide an identifying label.

☑ Label scrolling lists whenever possible and if they are not the only control in the window, especially when the purpose of the scrolling list is not obvious or when scrolling lists are grouped together.

☑ Position the label to the left of the scrolling list and align it with the first line of text in the scrolling list.

Figure 7-32 shows two scrolling lists with labels.

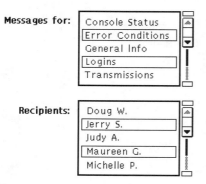

Figure 7-32   Examples of scrolling lists with labels.

Labeling for Exclusive and Nonexclusive Settings

Exclusive and nonexclusive settings fall naturally into groups.

☑   Provide labels for groups of exclusive and nonexclusive settings.

Figure 7-33 shows an example of a label for a group of nonexclusive settings.

Attributes: `Bold` `Italic` `Underscore`

Figure 7-33   Example of a labeled group of nonexclusive settings.

Figure 7-34 shows an example of a two-line label for a group of exclusive settings.

**When Exit
Is Requested:**

Save File Without Confirmation
Save File With Confirmation
Don't Save File

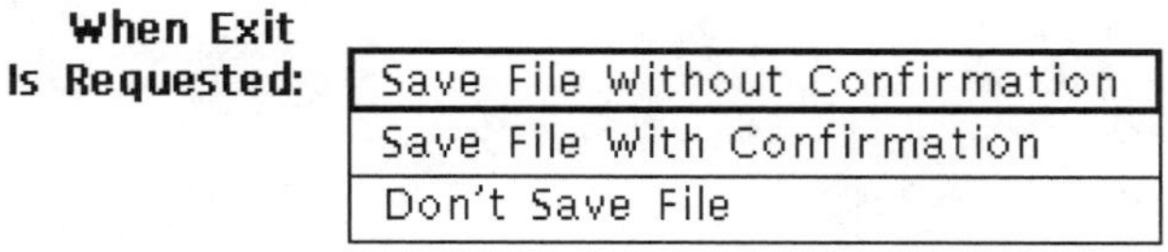

Figure 7-34 Example of a labeled group of exclusive settings.

Combining Titles and Labels Effectively

When controls have both titles and labels, you can combine them effectively in a number of different ways.

As an example, when users can choose whether they want to overwrite a file, you could present the information in a number of different ways. When setting categories are grouped together in a command or property window, it is generally better to label each choice specifically, as shown in Figure 7-35.

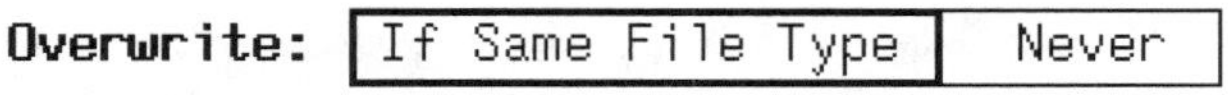

Overwrite: | If Same File Type | Never |

Figure 7-35 A good example of an unambiguous label and titles for an exclusive setting.

☑ Make the title of each control descriptive, when possible, so that users do not need to read both the label and the title to determine what control to choose.

Conversely, when you use check boxes, the entire burden of conveying the purpose for the control is borne by the label for the check box. You might be tempted to provide more explanatory information in a label for a check box. The example shown in Figure 7-36 is an example of a badly labeled control.

Users must read carefully to determine if they should put a check in the box for an affirmative response. Rewording the label could make it negative, in which case users would check the box if they did not want to overwrite the file.

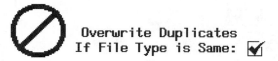

Figure 7-36 A badly designed label for a check box.

☑ Do not label exclusive settings as a two-state switch with Yes/No titles.

Suppose this same control is presented as a one-word label with Yes/No titles for exclusive settings, as shown in Figure 7-37. Users who are in the habit of answering Yes to a different kind of question might choose the Yes setting out of habit, not realizing the consequences of that choice in the current context.

Figure 7-37 A bad example of a label and text for exclusive settings.

This information could also be presented to users as a check box, as shown in Figure 7-38. Using a check box for this kind of a setting is not recommended, because there are serious consequences to users if they choose the wrong setting.

Figure 7-38 A bad example of a label and check box for yes/no information.

☑ Consider using nonexclusive settings for clarity whenever possible.

☑ Make the decision about whether to provide a check box or Yes/No settings based on consistency with other controls presented in the same control area.

☑ Consider how serious it is to users if they inadvertently choose the wrong option because of unclear wording or previously learned habits.

☑ Do not provide an isolated check box when all other controls in the window are exclusive or nonexclusive settings. If the control area has a number of check boxes and a small number of exclusive or nonexclusive settings, the check box is preferable.

Grouping Controls

☑ Group related controls so that users can find them easily.

The OPEN LOOK UI provides you with a number of ways to group controls:

☐ By giving each group its own heading

☐ By putting extra white space between each group

☐ By showing only one category at a time and providing a control that lets users switch between categories

White Space

The control area shown in Figure 7-39 separates buttons into appropriate groups, making them easier to read.

Figure 7-39 A good example of grouping related buttons in a control area.

☑ Use white space to distinguish groups of related controls in a control area, a pop-up window, or a menu.

Figure 7-40 shows the same control area without any white space. Packing a control area too densely with buttons makes it hard for users to pick out the desired button.

Figure 7-40 A bad example of a control area with no grouping of buttons.

Proper grouping of controls in menus can greatly improve their readability. Figure 7-41 shows an example of a menu with grouped items. See Chapter 8 for more information about menus.

Figure 7-41 A good example of using white space to group items in a menu.

Figure 7-42 shows an example of a property window that uses white space to distinguish groups of related controls.

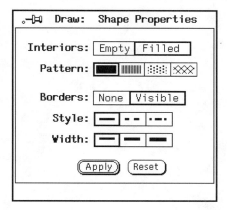

Figure 7-42   A good example of using white space to group related controls in a property window.

Headings for Groups of Controls

☑ If you need to make stronger distinctions between groups of controls, use headings to separate the related controls.

☑ Capitalize and bold the entire heading label. Do not underline it.

In the example shown in Figure 7-43, the properties are divided into two categories. Note that all of the letters of the headings are capitalized and bold to help users to pick the headings out when scanning the property window.

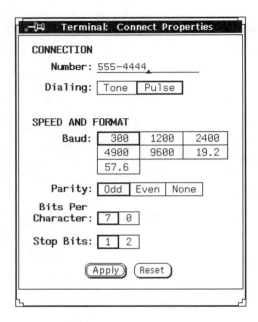

Figure 7-43   A property window with headings.

Grouping Controls by Categories

The more controls you present to users at once, the more likely they are to find the application complex or even intimidating. Furthermore, displaying too many settings at one time makes a window too large.

☑ When you are presenting many controls, group them into categories, and let users choose which category is displayed.

Grouping controls into categories is most effective in property windows.

☑ Apply changes when users switch between categories.

See Chapter 9 for guidelines about displaying Notices when users switch between categories.

Grouping with an Exclusive Setting

☑ To present categories of properties or commands, use an exclusive setting in the control area of the pop-up window when users do not need to see both sets of controls displayed at the same time.

Figure 7-44 shows a property window with an exclusive setting in the control area that permits users to switch between two categories.

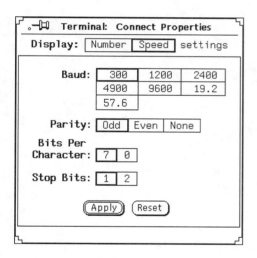

Figure 7-44 A property window with two categories.

When users choose the speed category, only the settings related to speed are displayed in the pane of the property window. When users choose the Number category, the contents of the pane show only settings related to

Number. The area of the property window changes to provide just enough space to display the requested settings.

Grouping with an Abbreviated Menu Button

☑ When you need to present more categories than will fit in the control area, group the categories together on a menu and attach that menu to an abbreviated menu button.

An abbreviated menu button shows users the current category and also allows them to display the menu to see all the possible categories at a glance.

The property window shown in Figure 7-45 is displaying settings for the Speed and Format category.

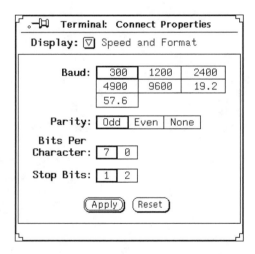

Figure 7-45 A property window with categories presented using an abbreviated menu button.

When you use an abbreviated menu button to display multiple categories, consider including a Next item in the menu to allow users to cycle through the categories by clicking SELECT on the menu button. An example of this convention is described later in this chapter in the section "Combining Controls."

☑ Use an abbreviated menu button when many categories need to be presented and/or the list is dynamic, and when only one category can be displayed at a time.

Grouping with Nonexclusive Settings

☑ When you have only a few categories and there are only a few controls in each category, use nonexclusive settings to let users choose how many categories to display at one time.

Figure 7-46 shows a property window that can be displayed in three configurations: With the Number category settings, with the Speed category settings, and with both Number and Speed settings.

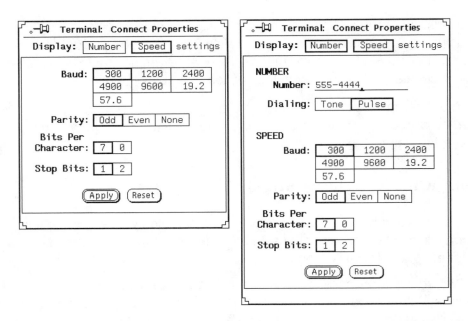

Figure 7-46 A property window with nonexclusive settings for choosing categories.

Other Category Variations

You can also present variations of categories with groups of exclusive settings, as shown in Figure 7-47, which is an example of a spreadsheet application. Two exclusive settings are provided opposite the Display label. The upper settings allow users to move quickly in the hierarchy from cell to region. The lower setting distinguishes between the format and the contents of the object.

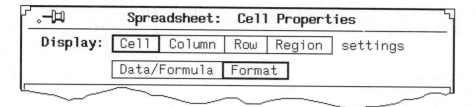

Figure 7-47 A property window with groups of exclusive settings for choosing
categories.

Combining Controls

This section shows examples of some of the most common ways to
combine the basic controls to form useful compound controls.

Cycle Menu Button

You can create a control that permits users to cycle through the list of
possible alternatives in the following way:

☐ Use an abbreviated menu button.

☐ Define the first item on the menu to be the command item "Next."

☐ Define exclusive settings for the rest of the controls on the menu.

Figure 7-48 shows an example of exclusive settings used with a Next command item to create a cycle control.

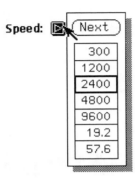

Figure 7-48   An abbreviated button menu with a Next command item and settings combined to form a cycle control.

The first control on a menu is, typically, the default. When Next is the default item, users can click SELECT on the abbreviated menu button to choose the default item without displaying the menu. By repeatedly clicking SELECT on the abbreviated menu button, users can cycle easily through all of the exclusive settings without needing to display the menu. The current setting is displayed to the right of the abbreviated menu button, so there is no ambiguity about which setting is current.

Alternatively, users can make one of the choices the default and can reset the setting to that choice at any time by clicking SELECT on the abbreviated menu button.

☑ Use an abbreviated menu button with a Next item on its menu as a convenient way for users to step quickly through a small list of settings.

Using Text Fields with Abbreviated Menu Buttons

You can display the current value next to an abbreviated menu button as a text field, as shown in the example in Figure 7-49.

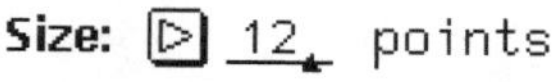

Size: ▷ 12 points

Figure 7-49 An abbreviated button menu used for standard point sizes.

Users could choose a point size from the button menu or type a value in the field and press RETURN to validate it.

☑   Use text fields with an abbreviated menu button when you want to allow users to enter frequently used values without needing to display a menu.

For example, an application may specify font sizes for 8, 10, 12, and 14 points on the menu but permit users to type in another font size value, such as 11, that is not provided on the menu.

Using Scrolling Lists with Abbreviated Menu Buttons

Sometimes you will have too many choices to fit into the menu of an abbreviated menu button. In that case, you can allow users to access a scrolling list by providing a window item on the menu. When users choose the window item, display a command window containing a scrolling list. You could get quite elaborate with this design. For example, you could allow users to customize the button menu using the scrolling list command window. Then users would have to choose Show List only when an infrequently accessed item was required.

Figure 7-50 shows an example of an abbreviated button menu that is used to open a command window containing a scrolling list.

Figure 7-50 An abbreviated button menu used to open a window with a scrolling list.

☑ Use a window item on an abbreviated button menu to display a scrolling list when there are too many choices to fit comfortably on the menu.

Annotating Controls with Read-only Text

You can use read-only text to present a control in a clear and succinct way. In the example shown in Figure 7-51, the text helps to clarify the label, defining the interpretation of the numbers in the setting. Without the read-only text, either the setting or the label would need to be more verbose.

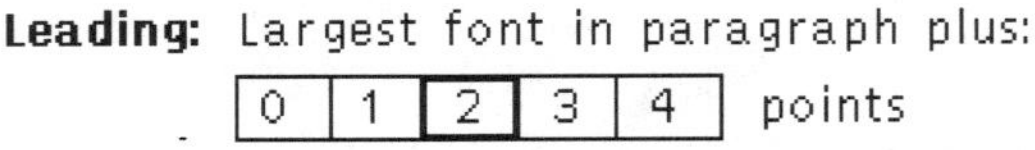

Leading: Largest font in paragraph plus:
　　　　　| 0 | 1 | 2 | 3 | 4 | points

Figure 7-51 Effective use of text to clarify a control.

☑ Use read-only text to clarify the meaning of complicated controls.

In general, it is a good idea to try to write clear and understandable labels rather than depending on read-only text.

Note that your toolkit might not explicitly permit you to create controls that look like the example in Figure 7-51. You may need to type the label and message above the setting as a read-only message and leave the label area next to the setting blank or fill it with spaces.

Using Text Fields with Settings

Often there are a few common values for a setting, but you want users to be able to enter other, less common values. In such situations, you can design for both simplicity and flexibility by combining an exclusive setting with a text field.

Figure 7-52 shows an example of an exclusive setting with a text field.

Leading: Largest font in paragraph plus:
| 0 | 1 | 2 | 3 | 4 | Other: | 8 | points |

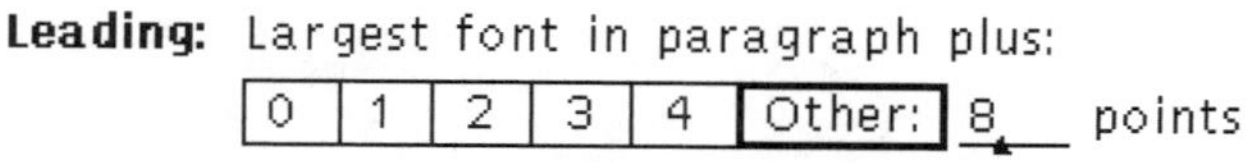

Figure 7-52 Effective combination of a setting and a text field.

When another setting is chosen, you can either make the text field inactive or remove it from the display. Showing an inactive control helps users interpret the controls that are active. Inactivating a control minimizes changes in a window. Showing and hiding controls can be distracting, particularly when the controls come and go frequently. Figure 7-53 shows the same controls with the text field inactive (top) and hidden (bottom).

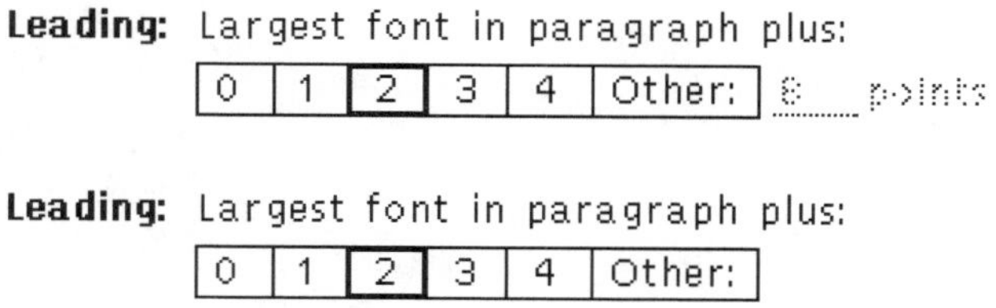

Leading: Largest font in paragraph plus:
| 0 | 1 | 2 | 3 | 4 | Other: | 8 | points |

Leading: Largest font in paragraph plus:
| 0 | 1 | 2 | 3 | 4 | Other: |

Figure 7-53 An inactive text field (top) and a hidden text field (bottom) when the setting is not chosen.

☑ Follow the title of the setting that activates the text field with a colon.

☑ When the setting is not chosen, inactivate the text field or hide it. Whichever method you use, be consistent throughout your application.

☑ If the controls are used infrequently, hide them when they are not chosen.

8

MENU CONFIGURATION

Menus are similar to cupboards in a kitchen, which provide a place to keep things handy yet out of the way. Menus in the OPEN LOOK Graphical User Interface provide a place for you to keep commands close by and convenient. Most housekeepers designate separate cupboards for different types of items, using one cupboard to store dishes and glasses, another to store pots and pans, and a third to store canned goods. In the same way, you design menus to store related groups of commands. Users want to be able to find commands easily and to access frequently used commands quickly.

This chapter provides a brief review of the types of menus in the OPEN LOOK UI and presents guidelines for good menu design. Because menus are an integral part of the OPEN LOOK UI, other information about menus is presented elsewhere in this book:

☐ See Chapter 3 for information about required OPEN LOOK UI menus and for a discussion of trade-offs for menus, controls, and pop-up windows.

☐ See Chapter 6 for recommended contents of the standard File, View, Edit, and Properties menus and for information about menu buttons.

☐ See Chapter 7 for information about menu titles and naming controls.

Types of Menus

Menus are ideal for presenting a small number of choices.

☑ Use menus for ten or fewer items.

By properly balancing the number, labels, and grouping of items in a menu, you can make the menu more efficient to use.

The OPEN LOOK UI provides for three kinds of menus:

☐ Button menus that are always attached to a menu button in a control area or pop-up window

☐ Pop-up menus that users access from a pane, from the window background, or from the workspace

☐ Submenus that users can access from either a button menu or a pop-up menu

Button Menus

Button menus are always attached to a menu button or an abbreviated menu button. Users identify the menu by the location and title of the menu button, which identifies the commands that are grouped on the button menu.

☑ Use button menus to group commands that are related to the menu button title.

For example, the commands on the standard File, View, Edit, and Properties menus are related to the title on the menu button.

Pop-up Menus

Pop-up menus provide users with a way to access frequently used commands that are available elsewhere in your application without needing to move the pointer out of the pane.

A pop-up menu for a pane is "prime real estate."

☑ Carefully consider what controls to put in pop-up menus.

The pop-up menu in Figure 8-1 is well designed: It is not too large, includes the most commonly used commands, and groups them logically.

Figure 8-1   A well-designed pop-up menu.

Use these guidelines when designing pop-up menus:

☑ Use pop-up menus in panes to complement, not replace, the menus and controls in the control area.

☑ Provide a subset of application controls that include only the most commonly used commands.

☑ Group the commands in the pop-up menu logically.

☑ Keep all of the controls at the first level when possible.

The pop-up menu shown in Figure 8-2 does not follow these guidelines. The Load and Show Title items are rarely used, and only one editing item (Delete) is included. In addition, the menu provides an item for rotating an object to the left but does not provide an item for rotating an item to the right.

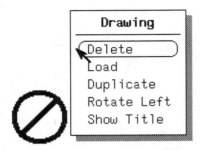

Figure 8-2   A poorly designed pop-up menu.

Figure 8-3 shows another example of a poorly designed pop-up menu. In this example, the designer has duplicated the entire control area on the pop-up menu. This design is not ideal, because a two-level menu makes it difficult for users to find the most commonly used commands quickly.

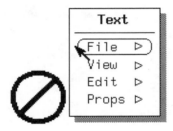

Figure 8-3   A bad example of a multi-level pop-up menu.

Submenus

Menus can contain menu items from which users can access submenus. Submenus are useful for grouping many items in a single menu; however, it is easy to overuse submenus. Each additional level makes the menu group more complex and less efficient.

☑ Limit menu groups to two levels whenever possible. Consider a pop-up window when a menu group becomes too large or unwieldy.

Figure 8-4 shows a menu group with two levels.

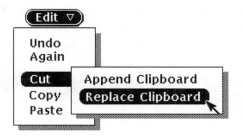

Figure 8-4   A two-level menu group.

The menu group shown in Figure 8-5 is a good candidate for redesign as a command or property window. If the settings affect an object for which users can request date-related properties, the setting belongs in a property window. If the function inserts a date into the document, it belongs in a command window.

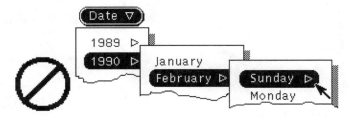

Figure 8-5   A poor use of submenus.

Designing Menus

The design of OPEN LOOK UI menus for your applications may well be the single most important design element in causing users to perceive your application as either easy and intuitive or frustrating and confusing. Good menu design provides logical grouping of commands into menus and submenus. Easy access can be provided by putting frequently used commands in pop-up menus and by putting pushpins on menus so that users can keep a favorite menu pinned to the workspace. This section contains guidelines for designing menus.

Grouping with White Space

The more controls a menu contains, the longer it takes users to locate and move the pointer to a desired item. Figure 8-6 shows an example of a menu group with the commands divided between two submenus.

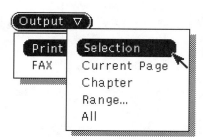

Figure 8-6   A menu divided into submenus.

Figure 8-7 shows the same menu with all the commands grouped on the primary menu. This menu contains too many items for users to scan at a glance, and the titles are poorly designed, using the same first word for each title in the group. When many items on a menu begin with the same first word, users will find it less useful to view the default without displaying the menu.

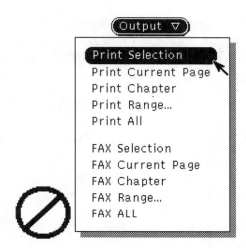

Figure 8-7   A poorly designed menu.

Proper grouping of menu controls can go a long way toward improving the readability of a menu. The absence of any grouping in Figure 8-8 is acceptable because the menu is short enough to scan.

Figure 8-8   A menu without groupings.

When groups of related items are separated by white space, as shown in Figure 8-9, users can tell at a glance which commands are related.

Figure 8-9 A good example of grouping of commands in a menu.

☑ Use white space between long groups of controls on menus or in short groups when screen real estate is not an issue.

Grouping with Columns

Separating menu items into columns is a good way to group related items and reduce mouse travel. Figure 8-10 shows an example of a multi-column menu.

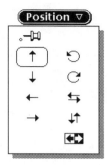

Figure 8-10 A multi-column menu.

☑ Use multi-column menus only with command items or when the menu contains only settings. Do not use multiple columns if the menu contains menu items.

Ordering Menu Items

☑ Order controls as a whole or within groups so that users can easily locate them.

☑ Use a logical order (if one exists) to help guide users through the process.

☑ Put most important or most frequently used functions at the top of the menu.

☑ When there is no particular usage order, alphabetize the controls.

For example, a menu might be arranged as follows: Index, Renumber, and Spell. Because there is no fixed order of use and users probably know the command for which they are searching, arranging these items alphabetically facilitates access.

☑ Put parallel functions in the same order within each grouping.

In the example shown in Figure 8-11, the Load and Save functions are the most important. Therefore, they are the first in the menu and are grouped together. Import and Export functions essentially load and save segments into a file, so they are grouped together and positioned next. Import (bring information in) is first, because it is parallel with Load (bring information in).

Figure 8-11   A menu with grouping and parallel construction.

In the example shown in Figure 8-12, the first column contains horizontal and vertical movements. Rotation and flipping functions are in the second column.

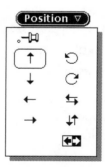

Figure 8-12   A menu that has glyph control items with grouping and parallel construction.

286

Choosing the Default for a Menu

As described previously, every OPEN LOOK UI menu, without exception, has a single default control. Users can change this default at any time while using the application.

☑ Specify an initial default for each menu in your application.

☑ Make the default the most commonly used item on the menu.

If you do not specify a default for a particular menu, the toolkit automatically makes the first item in the menu the default.

☑ Avoid choosing a default (such as Delete) that will have surprising or possibly destructive effects, even if it is a common operation. Remember that users can change the default.

When to Provide Pushpins for Menus

When a menu has a pushpin, users can pin the menu to the workspace, turning it into a pop-up window. The pinned menu can be moved to a convenient location and remains available until users dismiss it. Users pin up a menu by dragging the pointer onto the pushpin until it pops into the hole and releasing the MENU mouse button. The position submenu is dismissed and the menu becomes a pop-up window with a title and a Window menu. Users can reposition the pinned menu by dragging it. Figure 8-13 shows how users pin a menu.

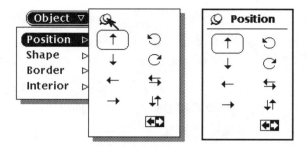

Figure 8-13 Pinning a menu.

☑️ Use a pushpin whenever a menu is used often enough that it makes sense for users to keep it open for repeated use.

The submenu shown in Figure 8-14 contains commands that operate on a region in a painting application. It is a good example of a submenu that needs a pushpin.

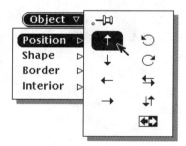

Figure 8-14 A submenu that requires a pushpin.

☑️ Submenus attached to a top-level menu are usually good candidates for a pushpin.

☑️ Do not provide pushpins for top-level menus whose only role is to display submenus or pop-up windows.

☑ When users pin a menu and when your toolkit does not automatically convert the title, use the button title or menu item title as the title of the pinned menu.

Maintaining State in Pinned Menus

Your application is responsible for tracking the state of a pinned menu and making sure that it is up to date. The most common example is activating and inactivating items in the Edit menu. Cut, Copy, and Delete should be inactive when there is no current selection, and Paste should be inactive when the clipboard is empty.

Ordinarily, checking these conditions whenever users display the menu is a simple matter. Once the menu is pinned, however, you can no longer tell when users need the commands. You must then assume the burden of keeping the state of the pinned menu up to date and synchronized with the state of the application as it changes.

☑ If, for some reason, an item that should be dimmed is not, and users choose that item, display a message in the footer of the window indicating that the action cannot be taken and the reason for that condition.

Giving Titles to Menu Controls

Giving menu controls a descriptive and logical title helps users to find controls that are hidden from view until a menu is displayed. The menu shown in Figure 8-15 shows a properly titled menu button with its menu commands.

Figure 8-15   Proper use of titles in menu commands.

Remember that the menu button acts as the title for the commands grouped on the button menu.

The menu in Figure 8-16 shows a menu button with a title that is the same as one of the commands on the menu. In this case, users might think the menu button title reflects the name of the default item when, in fact, it is a separate item.

Figure 8-16   A bad example of a menu button with a title that is the same as one of the commands on the menu.

☑   Never give a menu button the same title as one of the controls in its menu.

Unique Beginnings

Users can view the default from a button menu without displaying the menu by moving the pointer onto the menu button and pressing SELECT. For this information to be meaningful, the first word of each control on the menu must be unique.

Figure 8-17 shows a button that is displaying the default item, and the same button with the menu displayed.

Figure 8-17   Proper titling of items on a button menu.

When titles for controls all begin with the same word, viewing the default is much less useful, as shown in Figure 8-18.

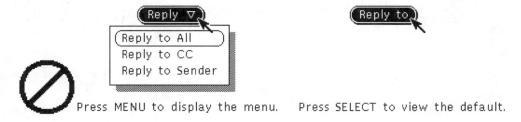

Figure 8-18   Improper titling of items on a button menu makes it useless to view the default.

291

Brief Versus Specific Titles

Another question to consider when choosing titles for controls in menus is how brief to be. You can generally find appropriate single-word labels, as shown in Figure 8-19.

Figure 8-19 A menu with single-word titles.

Using terse labels has two advantages: The commands are easier to scan, and the width of the menu is kept to a minimum. You may find it appropriate to make labels more descriptive. Figure 8-20 shows the same menu with more specific labels.

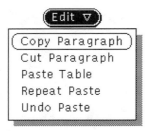

Figure 8-20 Titles can be more descriptive to convey specific information.

☑ Always label menu buttons with the type of command or option that the menu contains.

☑ Use brief and specific titles to make menus easier to scan.

☑ Expand titles on menus to make them more descriptive when an application is used infrequently or to remove ambiguity.

Showing a Binary State

Another design issue that frequently comes up is how to allow users to toggle between two states.

Suppose you are designing the interface for a CAD application in which users can turn a grid on and off. First you need to ask yourself whether the control for the grid belongs in a property window or on a menu. Assuming that you decide to put the control in a menu, you need to decide what type of control to use. As the menus in Figure 8-21 illustrate, you could use a nonexclusive setting, an exclusive setting, or a command.

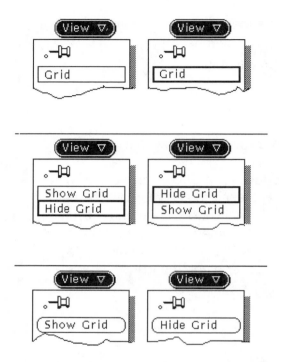

Figure 8-21   Three ways to present a two-state control.

Using either a command or a nonexclusive setting has two advantages:

☐ It is more compact because it requires only one line instead of two.

☐ When the item is the default, it allows users to toggle between the two states with a single click of the SELECT mouse button.

Glyphs in Menus

As discussed in Chapter 7, use glyphs with restraint.

☑   Use glyphs when the picture conveys useful information.

In the example shown in Figure 8-22, the arrows present useful functional information about the positioning of the graphic object.

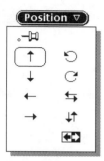

Figure 8-22 An appropriate use of glyphs in a menu.

The information conveyed is actually clearer than the commands would be if they were presented as text. The items on this menu, as text, represent the following commands, reading first down the left column and then down the right one:

□ Nudge right

□ Nudge left

□ Nudge up

□ Nudge down

□ Rotate clockwise

□ Rotate counterclockwise

□ Flip vertically

□ Flip horizontally

Sometimes, however, glyphs can be difficult to decipher. The glyphs on the menu shown in Figure 8-23 do not convey much useful information. In this case, titles would be more informative. It is difficult to determine, from these visual designs, what titles might be appropriate for each of these items.

Figure 8-23 An inappropriate use of glyphs in a menu.

☑ Use glyphs on menus with restraint, and only when the functional meaning is clear.

☑ Do not mix glyphs and text within the same menu.

9

MESSAGES

Introduction

It is essential that your application provide feedback about its state as users are working. The feedback of your application is similar to the kinds of feedback you get from appliances in your home. When the dryer has completed the drying cycle, it beeps. When you turn the oven on, an indicator light shows you it is on. On most electric ovens, another indicator light is on when the heating element is working and goes off to let you know when the specified temperature has been reached. If the power goes off, a VCR flashes the time indicator to let you know that it is no longer keeping proper time and that it may have lost its programming instructions.

This chapter provides guidelines for *message* feedback using the facilities provided by the OPEN LOOK Graphical User Interface. These messages can take the following forms:

☐ Messages that inform users of an ongoing condition, such as the name of a file that they are editing

☐ Informational messages (FYI) and messages that report on a particular situation

☐ Mode or state messages, such as page numbers or drawing modes

297

☐ Messages that cannot wait and that require users to take an action before they can continue working in the application

Messages from your application can be displayed in the footer of base and pop-up windows, in the header, and in Notices. Table 9-1 shows which types of messages are appropriate for each area.

Table 9-1   Message types and areas where they are displayed.

Message Type	Header	Left Footer	Right Footer	Notice
Condition messages	☑	☐	☐	☐
Informational messages	☐	☑	☐	☐
Mode or state messages	☐	☐	☑	☐
Can't wait message	☐	☐	☐	☑

General Message Guidelines

You can also categorize your messages by severity, in the following way:

☑ Use messages of low severity to provide general information, status, and mild warnings. Display these messages in the footer of the appropriate window without sounding the system bell.

☑ Use messages of medium severity to display errors that might not require immediate attention. Display these messages in the footer of the appropriate window.

☑ Use messages of high severity for circumstances that require immediate action. Display these messages in Notices that block input to the application.

When designing status and error messages, you need to decide how much is enough. It is impossible to give precise rules for how terse or verbose you should be with your messages. How you answer this question depends to some extent on personal preference as well as on whom you have in mind as target users.

Wording

☑ A consistent message "voice" is important.

Assume that the application is the implied subject for all messages generated by your application. For example, if users have typed incorrect information into a field, the message from the application is that (the application) "Cannot accept entry. CC is not a state."

☑ Use the following consistent format for all your error messages:
- ☑ Situation.
- ☑ Situation. Action.
- ☑ Situation. Reason.
- ☑ Situation. Reason. Action.

The situation tells users what is happening. The reason tells users why the situation has happened. The action tells users what to do about it. The following paragraphs provide examples for each type of message format.

When an application cannot find a specified file to load, the situation is that the application cannot find the file, and the following message is provided: "Cannot find file."

A database application that provides a message log for error reporting might post the following type of message, which describes the situation and suggests a course of action: "Server unavailable. See message log."

☑ Provide an action instruction only when your application can recommend a specific course of action.

☑ Write status, system, and error messages to sound as though they all come from the same person.

☑ Use terms users recognize. For example, "Establishing connection." is more readily understandable than the more technical term "Handshaking."

☑ Always use initial capital letters at the beginning of the message and a period at the end, even if the message is terse.

☑ Put two spaces after the period when it is followed by another sentence.

☑ Avoid assigning blame or offending users. Never accuse users of doing something wrong. Instead tell users why an action cannot be performed.

☑ Be polite. If you use the word "please" as part of your messages, be consistent.

☑ When your application cannot perform an action because it is dependent on some other operation that your application cannot control, inform users.

For example, when the application is unable to establish a connection to a server, let users know by displaying a message saying "Cannot connect. Server not responding."

☑ To keep messages as brief as possible, do not start a message with "The."

☑ When space permits, be as specific as possible to help users pinpoint a problem.

For example, if your application is unable to find a specific file, present the message in the following format: "Cannot find <filename>. Server not responding." However, if the file name will not fit in the message area, present the message in the following format: "Cannot find file. Server not responding."

☑ Avoid intimidating phrases such as "Fatal error." and "Operation aborted." They can be disconcerting to nontechnical users.

When to Scream and Shout

Be discreet in using the system bell. Too much beeping annoys users and is likely to cause them to disable the system bell from the Workspace Properties window.

☑ Sound the system bell once when displaying an important message.

☑ When displaying a series of messages, sound the bell for the first message in the set only.

☑ Sound the system bell if your application has the input area and discards a character without echoing it or performing some action based on it. This lets users know that the character has been ignored.

☑ When you post an error message for an icon, provide users with visual feedback that something has gone wrong by changing the icon image in some way. If you do not change the icon image, consider displaying a Notice if the error message is of appropriate severity.

Clearing Short-Term Messages

Clearing short-term messages when they no longer apply is every bit as important as displaying them in the first place.

☑ Leave short-term messages that recommend a user action displayed until users have completed the action.

☑ Consistently remove short-term messages after users click any mouse button or keyboard key in the pane that generated the message.

It may be tempting to leave a short-term message displayed until it is overwritten by the next message. This is not a good idea, because the message is likely to remain displayed long after the relevant situation has passed. Sooner or later, a scenario such as the following is likely to take place: A user, returning from a break, sees the message "Cannot load. File not found." and is unable to tell whether the message was left over from an earlier problem or was newly generated.

Providing Message Logs

☑ Consider keeping a record of status and error messages—a message log—if your application performs lengthy or complex operations consisting of a series of steps.

You can implement a message log as a scrollable text pane that is displayed either in a separate pop-up window or in the base window.

☑ Use a pop-up window to display a message log when an explicit action (such as a background process) generates messages that are of interest to your users.

If you use a pop-up window to display the message log, users can decide when and where to display the log and how big to make it. Put the command to display the message log in the View menu in the control area of the base window. Figure 9-1 shows an example of a message log. The message in the footer of the base window alerts users to the existence of the message log.

Figure 9-1   A message log in a pop-up window.

☑ Use the bottom of the base window or a resizable pop-up window to display a message log when almost everything the application does generates a message that users might want to see later.

Another place to put the message log is in a scrollable text pane at the bottom of the base window, as shown in Figure 9-2. Users can resize the window or pane to display more of the message log.

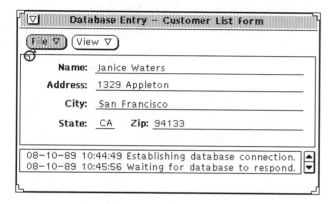

Figure 9-2   A message log at the bottom of a base window.

☑ Whether the message log is displayed in a pop-up window or in the base window, always provide a time stamp for messages so users know when they were generated.

☑ When you use one message log for multiple operations, always label the source operation for each message.

Printing the Message Log

☑ If you provide a message log, give users an easy way to print it.

☑ When you provide a message log in a command window, put a Print button in the command window.

☑ When you provide a message log in the base window, put a Message Log item on the Print submenu users access from the File menu in the control area of the base window.

Status Messages

The following sections provide guidelines for *long-term, medium-term,* and *short-term* status messages.

Long-Term Messages

The most common example of a long-term message is the name of the file being edited in a word processing, CAD, or spreadsheet application.

☑ Show the file or document name in the header of the base window following the application title, in bold font, separated from the title by an em dash (—) or two hyphens (--). Use the em dash if possible.

Figure 9-3 shows the header of a window followed by a file name.

Figure 9-3 A header with a document name following the application title.

☑ When you show the file or document name in the header, provide visual feedback so users can tell at a glance whether or not the document has been changed since it was last saved.

☑ Use parentheses around the file name to show the presence of unsaved edits.

Figure 9-4 shows the header of a window with a file name showing unsaved edits.

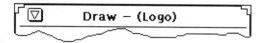

Figure 9-4   A header with a document name in parentheses to show that the file has been edited.

Medium-Term Messages

The OPEN LOOK UI specifies that the footer be divided into two regions. The left side of the footer is reserved for short-term messages. The right side of the footer is reserved for medium-term messages.

☑   Display status information, such as the current page or whether editing is enabled, on the right side of the footer of the base window.

☑   Make sure that messages that are displayed on the right side of the footer are brief.

Figure 9-5 shows the footer of a base window that displays the range of pages and the current page number for a document.

Figure 9-5   A medium-term status message on the right side of the footer.

Short-Term Messages

Short-term messages can be divided into the following categories:

☐ *Progress messages*

☐ *Completion messages*

☐ *Instruction messages*

All three of these types of status messages are positioned on the left side of the footer of the window.

☑ Keep users informed about the status or progress of operations of uncertain duration.

Typical examples include loading or saving a file, reorganizing a database, and searching for a text string. A good convention to use in such cases is to display the name of the operation, followed by three dots to indicate that the operation is in progress, as shown in Figure 9-6. Add an additional dot every one to ten seconds to show that the activity is still in progress. (You determine the appropriate interval at which to add new dots.) You can also use a follow-up sentence, such as "Contacting server. Please wait."

```
Saving file...
```

Figure 9-6   A status message followed by dots in a footer.

Multi-step Progress Messages

☑ Provide several progress messages for a lengthy multi-step process.

When considering such messages, ask yourself the following questions:

☐ Is it really necessary for users to be informed about each step of the process?

☐ Will a nontechnical user understand (or want to understand) the process?

Often a process can be broken down into many discrete steps from a technical standpoint. For example, connecting to a remote computer may require initializing a modem, dialing the phone number, waiting for the remote system to answer, recognizing the tone of the remote modem, verifying a password, and so on. If you display a new message for every step, the messages might flash by too quickly to be read, leaving users wondering what they missed. Even if messages are displayed long enough to be read, displaying trivial messages can condition users to ignore the message area.

☑ When you feel that it is important to signal each step of the process to users, it may be sufficient to use an updating message such as "Step # of #."

Figure 9-7 shows a multi-step progress message of this type.

Figure 9-7   A multi-step progress message.

Users can track the progress of the operation as your application updates the number from Step 2 of 5 to Step 3 of 5, and so on.

Completion Messages

☑ Completion messages are unnecessary when the effect of an operation is obvious.

For example, when users can see that a new file has been opened, a completion message is not needed.

☑ Post a completion message when an operation has far-reaching consequences that may not be immediately obvious.

For example, if users initiate a calculation in a spreadsheet that affects cells that might not be visible in the window, display a message such as "50 cells affected."

☑ When you provide progress messages, make sure users know when the process is complete.

☑ Replace a multi-step message with an appropriate completion message.

Figure 9-8 shows a stand-alone completion message.

Figure 9-8   A stand-alone completion message.

You can add a completion message following a three-dot progress message. In the example shown in Figure 9-9, the word "Done" is displayed when the process is completed.

Figure 9-9   A completion message that follows a progress message.

☑ Post a completion message for lengthy background operations.

Sometimes a completion message is called for even in the absence of a progress message. For example, if users initiate a Print operation that runs in the background, a progress message is inappropriate because it would interfere with other messages that might be displayed as users continue to work. In some environments, especially when printers are not located nearby, a completion message can be extremely helpful. You could post a completion message in the footer of the base window, like "Printing of <name of document> complete." Alternatively, you could provide printing functions from a command window and display printing status and completion messages in the footer of the command window.

☑ Consider providing a user option for sounding the system bell with completion messages for lengthy processes.

If it is likely that users will move on to other tasks while a lengthy process is being performed, consider providing a user option for sounding the system bell when you think users would want to be notified that the process is complete. Remember that audible feedback is normally reserved for important messages.

Incomplete Actions

☑ Always post an error message in the footer to notify users when an action cannot be completed or display a Notice for urgent situations.

Instruction Messages

☑ Use the short-term message area to give brief instructions to users, when appropriate.

For example, you can tell users exactly how to create each type of object in a drawing application. In the example shown in Figure 9-10, users have chosen the rectangle from the palette of drawing tools. The mode message at the right of the footer tells users that the rectangle tool is chosen. The instruction message at the left of the footer tells users how to proceed.

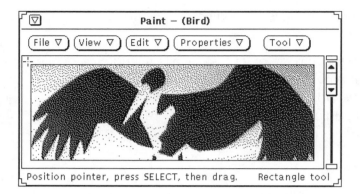

Figure 9-10   Instruction and mode messages working together.

Note that instruction messages can be annoying to experienced users.

☑ You may want to provide a setting in the application property window
that permits users to either enable or suppress the display of instruction
messages.

Sometimes an instruction message makes sense as the logical follow-up to
a completion message, as shown in Figure 9-11.

Figure 9-11   Completion and instruction messages working together.

Message Truncation

When users resize a window to make it narrower, the toolkit automatically
truncates messages to fit in the available space. Some toolkits add a
right-pointing dimmed More arrow at the end of the message to show that it
has been truncated.

☑ When your toolkit does not automatically truncate messages when a window is resized, provide message truncation and a More arrow for your application.

When there are two messages in the footer, the message on the right takes precedence over the short-term message on the left. First the message on the left is truncated, and then, if necessary, the message on the right is truncated.

Error Messages

☑ Display routine error messages indicating to users that an operation has failed or has irreversible consequences.

☑ Display error messages for the following types of actions:

☑ When users type invalid information into a text or numeric field
☑ When properties cannot be applied
☑ When an operation cannot be undone
☑ When users quit a window with unsaved edits
☑ When the operation will overwrite an existing file

You can display error messages in the following places:

☐ In the footer of the window that generated the message
☐ In a separate window
☐ In Notices

Displaying Validation Messages in the Footer

Error-checking frequently results in error messages to inform users that the information is incomplete or invalid. An appropriate example of this kind of error message is one your application would provide when the input of a text or numeric field cannot be validated.

Suppose you have a forms-based application for which you restrict input to a text or numeric field to a set of legal values, such as abbreviations for states or numbers within a certain range in a numeric field. When users indicate that input is finished by moving to a different field, your application validates the new input.

☑ If the input fails the validation test, use the short-term message area to display an appropriate error message.

Figure 9-12 shows an error message for invalid input.

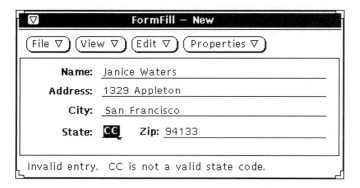

Figure 9-12   An error message for invalid text input.

Your application should force the input area to remain in the invalid field and should automatically select the contents of the field. Then users can immediately type the correction, because the selected text is deleted as soon as new input is received.

☑ When validating a single character, as opposed to a multi-character string, validate the character immediately, without waiting for users to move to a different field. When the character fails the test, display the error message, sound the system bell, and highlight the invalid character in the field.

Dismissal of Pinned Pop-up Windows

☑ When the operation initiated from a pop-up window fails, display the error message in the footer of the pop-up window and do not dismiss the window even if it is unpinned.

Figure 9-13 shows a command window after a failed load operation. Note that the pushpin is out, meaning that if the operation had been successfully completed, the window would have been dismissed automatically.

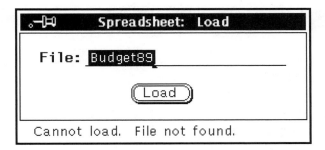

Figure 9-13 An error message in the footer of a command window.

☑ Use the footer of the property window to display an error message when the Apply operation fails for any reason.

Figure 9-14 shows an example of a property window with an error message in the footer.

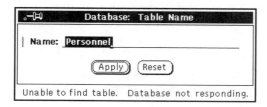

Figure 9-14   An error message in the footer of a property window.

Displaying Messages in a Separate Window

☑ Use another window to display error messages and legitimate alternatives for complicated validation procedures.

When an entire form is validated at once, several error messages might be generated.

When all the messages cannot fit into the message area, you can use one of the following techniques:

☑ When your application can present users with legitimate entries for a field, display abbreviated buttons in the fields.

If your toolkit supports glyphs inside abbreviated buttons, use a question mark or some other recognizable symbol. Users could click on the abbreviated button to display a command window that shows the valid possible entries for the field. If the field contained a two-letter abbreviation for a state name, the command window could display a list of the state abbreviations that your application considers valid for that field.

☑ As an alternative to abbreviated buttons, and if your toolkit can support it, put a noticeable symbol in the fields that require attention.

This symbol could be a large or highlighted question mark. Users could position the pointer over each symbol and press the Help key to display help for each item.

☑ When the invalid input is first flagged, display a message in the footer informing users of the situation and providing a method for resolution.

The message might take the following form: "Problems with 7 fields. Click on error symbols for details."

Displaying Messages in Notices

☑ Use Notices ONLY for serious warnings and error messages to which users must respond before proceeding.

While a Notice is displayed, it blocks all other user input to the application. Unneeded display of Notices in your application can be aggravating to users.

The most common use of Notices is to ask users to confirm an operation that cannot be undone, such as loading a file in the presence of unsaved edits or storing a file over an existing file of the same name.

Figure 9-15 shows the standard form of a confirmation Notice.

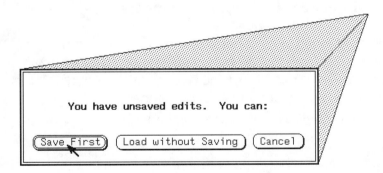

Figure 9-15 A standard confirmation notice.

☑ Do not use Notices to report on a situation.

Never use a Notice as an acknowledgment of an action, as shown in Figure 9-16. Single-button Notices such as this interrupt and irritate users and require unneeded acknowledgment. The appropriate way to present this information is as a completion message in the footer of the appropriate window.

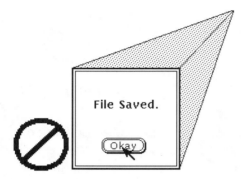

Figure 9-16   A bad example of a Notice.

Notices for Unapplied Changes in a Property Window

☑ When users change categories in a property window and the settings have not been applied, display a Notice with the message "Changes to this category have not been applied." Provide buttons titled "Apply Changes" (the default), "Discard Changes," and "Cancel."

☑ Use change bars to show settings that have been changed but not yet applied.

Using a Notice when users switch between categories allows users to apply changes for individual categories without needing to pin the property window. Otherwise, users would need to pin the window, apply changes for each category, and then switch to a new category.

Using the Help Window

Unless you implement a scrolling text pane for your message area, short-term footer messages are limited to a single line.

☑ When you provide additional help for display in the Help window, post a short-term message in the footer of the window, and mention that more help is available.

☑ When you need to provide more information than will fit in the footer of a window, use the standard Help window to provide additional information.

10

USING COLOR

This chapter provides a brief introduction to the use of color in designing applications for the OPEN LOOK Graphical User Interface. Topics include:

☐ Use of color in the interface background
☐ Guidelines for designing with color

See the References list for further suggested reading.

Using Color in the Interface Background

The use of color in the OPEN LOOK UI is based on the fundamental distinction between foreground and background. When you stand back and look at the workspace, the panes in which the application displays its information should stand out in the foreground. As the application designer, you specify how color is used within these panes.

The surrounding regions that contain the standard elements of the user interface form the interface background, which includes the background of the base window (with any controls it contains, such as resize corners, buttons, and scrollbars) and property and command windows in their entirety.

In the OPEN LOOK UI, the color of the interface background is specified by users, not the application designer. Users control the color of the interface background by choosing colors from palettes, as described in the next section.

Palettes

A palette is a set of colors that go well together; palettes are provided by the toolkit. Because displays differ greatly in color capabilities, the toolkit must supply palettes designed specifically for the type of display that the toolkit is using.

Providing palettes of related colors accommodates individual tastes while ensuring that the overall effect is pleasing and readability is not degraded.

Each palette consists of three subpalettes, one for each of the following regions:

☐ The workspace background

☐ The window backgrounds

☐ The current selection

Workspace Background

The workspace, as the true background of the scene, has the most neutral color.

Window Background

For the purposes of coloring, the controls in a base window control area or a pop-up window pane are treated as part of the window background. The window background has a dual position. Although it is part of the foreground with respect to the workspace, it is part of the background in relation to the application information.

The palettes for the window backgrounds contain neutral, lightly saturated colors so as not to overwhelm the information presented in the pane of an application.

A single background color is used for all the windows of a given application so that users can tell at a glance which windows go with which application. Users specify the background color as one of the base window properties.

Current Selection

The current selection is in the foreground of the visual scene. Because the selection is the object of users' immediate attention, the palette for the current selection is composed of bright, highly saturated colors.

Using Color in Controls

In a three-dimensional implementation, shading is used to give controls the illusion of depth. The top and left borders are rendered in white, and the bottom and right borders are rendered in a darker shade of the background color.

When users press a button, the light and dark borders are reversed, and the interior of the button is darkened, giving the illusion that the button has actually been pushed into the surface.

Using Color in Icons

The icon background has the same color as the window background. The glyph and the text in the icon are rendered in black. You can override this standard use of color for the purpose of color-coding icons.

Guidelines for Designing with Color

This section offers some general guidelines for using color in user interfaces.

Design for Monochrome First

☑ Design your entire interface for a monochrome system if your application is to run on both color and monochrome systems.

The use of color cannot repair a design that is incoherent in black and white. On the contrary, the addition of color is likely to make a poor design worse.

Another reason to avoid basing your design exclusively on color is that people vary in their abilities to distinguish colors. For example, 8 percent of men cannot distinguish between red and green. A smaller percentage have trouble distinguishing between blue and yellow. Many people who are not considered to have a color perception deficiency see the distinctions between blue and green differently. It is not a good idea to rely on users' ability to distinguish between these colors.

Use Color Purposefully

☑ Always ask yourself whether using color in a particular setting will make the interface easier to use.

☑ Use color to control the eye path and focus of attention.

The eye is drawn to an area of color in a sea of black and white, or to a bright color against a background of pale colors.

☑ Confine the use of color for marketing splash and sizzle to places where color coding is unimportant, such as power-up and log-on screens.

Use Color Sparingly

☑ To use color with purpose, be sure to exercise restraint.

If you use too many colors (particularly too many highly saturated colors), the distinction between background and foreground becomes blurred. Undisciplined use of color can result in a chaotic effect.

Color Coding

Any time color is used purposefully to convey a specific message, it is acting as a "code." The color coding examples presented in Table 10-1 are from the book *Human-Computer Interface Design Guidelines* (Brown, C.M., Ablex-Publishing, 1988).

Table 10-1   Examples of color coding.

Color	Use
White/black	Base color
Red	Alarms or errors; Stop
Yellow	Warnings or data that may require attention
Green	Normal or okay; Go; Base color if white is too bright
Saturated blue	De-emphasis, shading; not for critical data
Pink (magenta)	Secondary alarm color, differentiating data
Turquoise (cyan)	Differentiating data types
Other colors	Differentiating data types

Limit the Number of Codes

Remember that each individual color code has to be identified and interpreted by users. With each additional color code, the time it takes to identify the code is increased and the accuracy decreases.

☑ As a rule of thumb, never use more than seven color codes in total, and never show more than four codes on the screen at one time.

You can, however, use saturation and shades of these four to seven colors without considering them separate colors.

Cultural Associations

For Westerners, red generally has a negative connotation and can be used effectively as a code to mean "stop," "error," "hot," "danger," and so on. Other cultures have different associations. For example, in China, red connotes happiness. Make an attempt to know what associations your users bring with them as they approach your application.

Industry Conventions

Many disciplines that use computers have their own conventions for color coding. Circuit designers, for example, use colors to distinguish layers on board designs. Resistors are color-coded to show their value. Color codes are often used in architectural floor plans.

☑ Follow industry color conventions when appropriate.

Interactions Between Neighboring Colors

When choosing a color for a particular area, it is important to be aware of the ways in which neighboring colors interact.

Canceling Like Attributes

When two colors are placed next to each other, the effect is to de-emphasize the like attributes of each color and to exaggerate the dissimilar attributes. For example, when an area of orange is placed beside an area of green, the yellow attributes of the two colors tend to cancel each other. The result is that the green looks more blue, and the orange looks more red.

Colors at the opposite ends of the spectrum, such as red and blue, produce a vibrating effect when placed next to each other. The more saturated the colors are, the worse the effect. Red text on a blue background is very difficult to read.

☑ Avoid putting colors at opposite ends of the spectrum next to one another.

Halation

Black on white is more readable than white on black, due to an effect known as *halation.* Halation refers to the glow or halo-like effect of ambient light around brightly lit objects placed against a dark background. On a CRT, halation causes a white (or very light) pixel on a dark background to appear larger than a dark pixel on a light background. Thus, when white characters appear on a black background, they tend to "glow" around the edges and become indistinct.

Blurring

☑ Never put two small areas of saturated color that must be clearly distinguished next to each other.

For example, a one-pixel yellow line beside a one-pixel blue line tends to be perceived as a two-pixel green line.

Consider the Size of the Object

The larger the object, the less it demands saturated colors. Large areas of highly saturated color tend to lead to after-images and eye fatigue. The background of a pane, for example, should be colored in a muted pastel shade if it is colored at all.

Color for Low-resolution Displays

Low-resolution displays do not have lightly saturated colors. This makes the design of color interfaces on low resolution systems much more difficult.

☑ Use colors even more sparingly on a low-resolution display, because the highly saturated colors can easily distract users.

Appendix A

CERTIFICATION

The right to use the OPEN LOOK trademark is subject to a certification procedure. For detailed information about the certification procedure, see the *OPEN LOOK Graphical User Interface Trademark Guide,* available from AT&T, OPEN LOOK GUI Trademark Quality Control Manager, 60 Columbia Turnpike, Room 129B-A208, Morristown, NJ 07962, telephone (201) 829-8996.

To facilitate implementation, the functionality of the OPEN LOOK Graphical User Interface is divided into three levels:

□ Level 1 is a complete user interface, containing all the essential features. This is the minimum feature set required for a toolkit to be certified as compliant with Level 1.

□ Level 2 is a superset of Level 1. It is anticipated that this level will be the most common level of compliance. The complete set of Level 2 features must be provided for an implementation to be certified as compliant with Level 2.

□ Level 3 is a superset of Level 2. This level is provided for more specialized features and to provide a mechanism for extending the functionality of the OPEN LOOK UI.

Alphabetized lists of the main features in each level are presented in the following sections.

Level 1

Basic window types: base, Command, Property, Help, and Notice windows
Control areas with:

☐ Button controls
☐ Abbreviated menu buttons
☐ Exclusive and nonexclusive settings
☐ Text fields (scrollable)
☐ Basic horizontal sliders
☐ Check boxes

Icons
Menus

☐ Both press-drag-release and stay-up modes
☐ Controls of the same kind: items, exclusive or nonexclusive settings
☐ Optional pushpins

Mouse/Keyboard

☐ Mouse buttons: SELECT, ADJUST, MENU
☐ Mouse modifiers: DUPLICATE, PAN, CONSTRAIN, SETMENUDEFAULT
☐ Core functions: COPY, CUT, HELP, PASTE, PROPERTIES, UNDO
☐ Pop-up accelerators: DEFAULTACTION, CANCEL
☐ Text Field Navigation: NEXTFIELD, PREVFIELD

Pointer jumping (with preference to disable)

Pointers

□ Basic pointer

□ Busy pointer

□ Duplicate pointer

□ Move pointer

□ Question mark pointer

□ Text duplicate pointer

□ Text move pointer

Scrollbars

□ Basic scrollbar

□ Scrollbar without cable

□ Abbreviated scrollbar

□ View need not be updated while elevator is dragged

□ Vertical or horizontal

□ Scrollbar menus

Scrolling lists

□ Basic

□ Support text only

Window management

□ Windows and icons are selectable

□ Selected windows/icons are moved as a group

OPEN LOOK GUI Application Style Guidelines

Window menus (base and pop-up)

Window properties

☐ Initial location

☐ Initial state (icon or window)

☐ Initial size

☐ Record current base window state

Workspace properties

☐ Color
  ▫ Workspace
  ▫ Windows
  ▫ Selection

☐ Icons
  ▫ Location

☐ Keyboard core functions
  ▫ COPY
  ▫ CUT
  ▫ HELP
  ▫ PASTE
  ▫ PROPERTIES
  ▫ UNDO

☐ Keyboard miscellaneous functions
  ▫ CANCEL
  ▫ DEFAULTACTION
  ▫ NEXTFIELD
  ▫ PREVFIELD

☐ Menus
- ▫ Drag-right distance

☐ Miscellaneous
- ▫ System beeping

☐ Mouse modifiers
- ▫ SELECT
- ▫ ADJUST
- ▫ MENU
- ▫ NONE
- ▫ DUPLICATE
- ▫ PAN
- ▫ CONSTRAIN
- ▫ SETMENUDEFAULT

☐ Mouse settings
- ▫ Enable/disable scrollbar pointer jumping
- ▫ Enable/disable pop-up pointer jumping

☐ Programs submenu
- ▫ Editable scrolling list

Level 2

Abbreviated buttons

Basic window types: nonstandard

Blocking pop-up windows

Borderless icon setting for color implementations

Change bars in property windows

Clipboard

☐ Clipboard item on Workspace Utilities menu
☐ Ability to append to the clipboard

Color

Controls

☐ Multi-line text areas
☐ Edit menu for text fields
☐ Numeric text fields with increment/decrement buttons
☐ Read-only gauges

File Manager

Menus containing more than one type of control

Mouse/keyboard

☐ Core functions
   ▫ STOP

☐ Accelerators and modifiers
   ▫ ADJUST
   ▫ CHARBAK

- CHARFWD
- DECHARBAK
- DELCHARFWD
- DELLINEBAK
- DELLINE
- DELLINEFWD
- DELWORDBAK
- DELWORDFWD
- DOCEND
- DOCSTART
- LINEEND
- LINESTART
- MENU
- NEXTWINDOW
- PAGE
- PANEEND
- PANESTART
- POINTERDOWN
- POINTERLEFT
- POINTERRIGHT
- POINTERUP
- PREVWINDOW
- ROWDOWN
- ROWUP
- SCROLLBOTTOM
- SCROLLDOWN
- SCROLLLEFT
- SCROLLLEFTEDGE
- SCROLLRIGHT
- SCROLLRIGHTEDGE
- SCROLLTOP
- SCROLLUP
- SELECT

- □ SELCHARFWD
- □ SELLINEFWD
- □ SELWORDFWD
- □ TOGGLEINPUT
- □ UNSELCHARBAK
- □ UNSELINEBAK
- □ WORDFWD
- □ WORDBAK

Panes

- ☐ Resizable
- ☐ Selectable
- ☐ Splittable

Pointers

- ☐ Panning pointer
- ☐ Target pointer

Scrollbars

- ☐ Minimum scrollbar
- ☐ View must be updated while elevator is dragged
- ☐ Page-oriented option
- ☐ Split View and Join Views items on Scrollbar menu

Scrolling

- ☐ Automatic scrolling
- ☐ Panning

Scrolling lists

- ☐ Glyphs in scrolling lists

☐ Hierarchical

Sliders

☐ End boxes
☐ Tick marks
☐ Vertical sliders

Soft function keys
Text

☐ Dragging text to move/copy
☐ Quick Move and Quick Duplicate on text

Window manager

☐ Constrained move/resize of windows/icons
☐ Pop-up control panel for operating on selected windows/icons

Window properties

☐ Base window scale
☐ Pop-up window scale
☐ Manage Windows settings
☐ Record Current State buttons for base window, pop-up window, and menus

Workspace properties

☐ Icons
  ▫ Border
  ▫ Align to grid
  ▫ Grid origin
  ▫ Grid spacing

☐ Keyboard core functions
 ▫ STOP

☐ Menu
 ▫ MENU mouse click

☐ Miscellaneous
 ▫ Scale at startup
 ▫ Set input area
 ▫ SELECT always brings window forward

☐ Workspace menu replaces the Programs Submenu category. A hierarchical scrolling list permits editing of all levels of the Workspace menu.

Level 3

Process Manager

Appendix B

WRITING ABOUT THE OPEN LOOK GRAPHICAL USER INTERFACE

Introduction

This appendix contains the following information:

☐ The correct usage for the OPEN LOOK trademark

☐ Issues to consider when you decide on the audience for your documentation

☐ A narrative description of general elements of the OPEN LOOK user interface

☐ Style guidelines

The Glossary in this book contains a list of terms and definitions for each of the elements of the OPEN LOOK UI. Use this appendix in conjunction with the terminology and definitions in the Glossary.

Correct Usage of the OPEN LOOK Trademark

The name OPEN LOOK is a trademark of AT&T. The first time you use the name OPEN LOOK, it must have the trademark symbol (OPEN LOOK™). Subsequent uses of the OPEN LOOK name need not display the trademark symbol.

OPEN LOOK GUI Application Style Guidelines

Never use the term OPEN LOOK as a noun. It must always used as a modifier to a specific product. When there is no specific product, OPEN LOOK must always be followed by the initials GUI or UI. The following list shows some acceptable examples:

☐ OPEN LOOK graphical user interface (OPEN LOOK GUI)
☐ OPEN LOOK user interface (OPEN LOOK UI)
☐ OPEN LOOK end user system (or system)
☐ OPEN LOOK toolkit
☐ OPEN LOOK window manager
☐ OPEN LOOK workspace manager
☐ OPEN LOOK file manager

The following list shows some specific terms that require the initials GUI or UI following the name OPEN LOOK:

☐ OPEN LOOK UI guidelines
☐ OPEN LOOK UI conventions
☐ OPEN LOOK UI implementation
☐ OPEN LOOK UI environment

Basic Assumptions

Any time you write about the OPEN LOOK UI, be sure to evaluate your basic assumptions about the audience you are addressing. The following list suggests some issues to consider:

☐ Users may be familiar with computers, but not with the use of a mouse.
☐ Users may be familiar with the use of a mouse, but need specific information about how mouse buttons are used in the OPEN LOOK UI.
☐ Users may be familiar with an environment with just one active application.

☐ Users may be familiar with a PC windowing environment in which only one window is active.

☐ Users may be familiar with a multitasking windowing environment in which all windows are active when they are opened, but not when they are displayed as icons.

☐ Users may be familiar with a multitasking windowing environment in which all windows are active whether they are open or closed to an icon.

☐ Users may have different levels of operating system knowledge and experience.

The Basic Environment

This section provides a narrative general description of the OPEN LOOK UI. Specific OPEN LOOK UI terms are shown in *italics* the first time they are used.

The OPEN LOOK UI windowing environment is referred to as the *workspace*. The workspace has its own menu from which users can start applications or customize specific global elements of their workspace environment.

Windows and Window Elements

Applications display their information inside of *windows*. A *base window* can be closed into an *icon*. The application is still active when it is displayed as an icon, and may continue running processes. When an icon is *opened*, it is replaced with its window, which is displayed in the same position it occupied before users closed it. The term "icon" is reserved for the closed representation of a window. Refer to any other graphic object or picture as a *glyph* or *image*. Figure B-1 shows a typical icon.

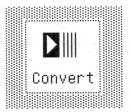

Figure B-1 A typical icon.

The primary window for an application is the base window. Typical applications have one base window, but some applications may have several base windows. Any base window can be closed and displayed on the workspace as an icon. Figure B-2 shows a typical base window with its elements labeled.

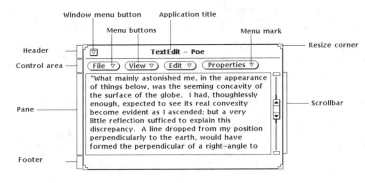

Figure B-2 A typical base window.

Most applications also use *pop-up windows* to display information or to provide a way for users to enter commands. When the commands are executed, the pop-window is dismissed and is removed completely from the screen.

The four kinds of pop-up windows are:

☐ *Command* window

☐ *Help* window

☐ *Property* window

☐ *Notice*

Figure B-3 shows a typical command window.

```
 .─🔲        TextEdit: Search and Replace

        Find: ◈────────────────────────────────

Replace with: _____

     Options: │ Confirm Each │    │ Ignore Case │

        ( Search Forward )  ( Search Backward )

```

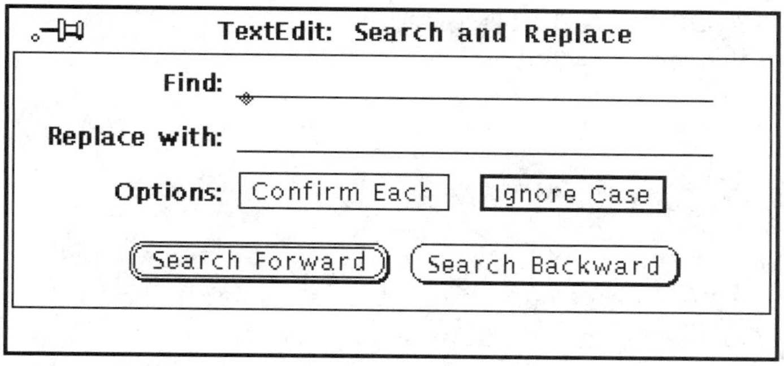

Figure B-3   A typical command window.

Each window has a *header*, the area at the top. When the window has the *input area*, the header *highlights*. The header contains a *Window menu button* for base windows and a pushpin for all pop-up windows except Notices.

The pushpin can be either *pinned* or *unpinned*. Clicking SELECT on a pinned pushpin dismisses the pop-up window. The header also contains the title of the application and may contain a *long-term message*, such as the name of a file.

Resize corners allow users to adjust the area of a window.

Many windows have a *control area* with *buttons* or other controls. The most common controls in a control area are buttons. Buttons perform one of three functions:

☐ *Activate* a command: *command buttons*

☐ *Display* a pop-up window: *window buttons*

☐ *Display* a menu: *menu buttons*

Windows also have *panes*, which are rectangular, nonoverlapping areas in which application data are displayed. When the view of the data in a pane can be adjusted by users, the pane has a *scrollbar*. See "Scrolling Actions" later in this appendix for scrollbar and scrolling terminology.

Many windows have a *footer* that is used for the display of status, error, state, or mode messages.

Users can *select* windows and icons and perform multiple operations on them from a *Window Controls pop-up*. When a window or icon is selected, the border *thickens* or is bold. Some panes can also be selected.

The Mouse or Pointing Device

The OPEN LOOK UI is designed to be used with a *pointing device*. This device is usually a three-, two-, or one-button mouse. Users may, however, have some other kind of pointing device, such as a track ball or a digitizing tablet with a stylus. A Level 2 implementation allows users to assign mouse functions to function keys on the keyboard. Be sure to write descriptions that are appropriate to the pointing device. When you do not know the specific hardware environment, or when many environments are possible, use generic descriptions.

The default mapping of mouse buttons on a three-button mouse is:

☐ *SELECT* for LEFT

☐ *ADJUST* for MIDDLE

☐ *MENU* for RIGHT

Users can customize the mouse button assignments as well as assign them to function keys on the keyboard from the *Workspace Properties window*. Because you cannot know how users have customized the mouse functions, you should always use the logical name for the mouse button rather than its location on the mouse. Say "Click the SELECT mouse button" or, as a shortcut, "Click SELECT."

Use the following terms to describe actions performed with the mouse:

☐ *Press* a mouse button and hold it.

☐ *Release* a mouse button to initiate the action.

☐ *Click* a mouse button by pressing and releasing it before you move the pointer.

☐ *Double-click* a mouse button by clicking twice quickly without moving the pointer.

☐ *Move* the pointer by sliding the mouse with no buttons pressed.

☐ *Drag* the pointer by sliding the mouse with one or more buttons pressed.

☐ *Point* to a control or an object by moving the pointer to the appropriate place on the screen.

The Input Area

When users can type characters from the keyboard into a field or pane, that window has the current input area.

Users set the place where characters are displayed by clicking SELECT or ADJUST to set the *insert point*. When users release the mouse button, the header of the window is highlighted and the *active caret* is displayed. Input areas include text panes, single-line text fields commonly found in control areas, pop-up windows, and tables. The *caret* shows users the exact place where characters typed from the keyboard are inserted into the text area. When the input area shifts to a different window, the caret changes shape, is *dimmed*, and becomes *inactive*.

Menus

Menus provide additional control areas that are hidden from view until users display them.

There are three types of menus:

☐ *Button menus*

☐ *Pop-up menus*

☐ *Submenus*

Each region of the screen in an OPEN LOOK UI implementation that is not covered by a control has a menu. When the pointer is on a menu button and the user presses MENU, the menu for that button is displayed. When the pointer is on any other area of the screen, the pop-up menu that is displayed depends on the location of the pointer. Submenus are always accessed from another menu. A menu and its associated submenus are called a *menu group*.

Menus have *settings* and/or lists of *items* with which users can issue commands or display a submenu with additional controls. Menu items have the same "feel" as buttons but have a different "look." Items that have a *window mark* (...) are used to display a pop-up window. Items that have a *menu mark* (a hollow triangle) are used to display submenus. When the menu is first displayed, the default item has a *default ring* around it. When the pointer is on an item, the item is highlighted. When the mouse button is released, the command is activated and the menu or menu group is dismissed. Figure B-4 shows how users choose from a menu.

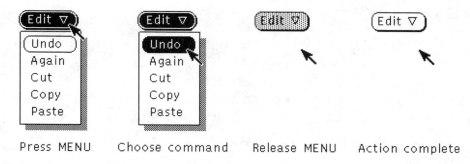

Press MENU   Choose command   Release MENU   Action complete

Figure B-4   Choosing from a menu.

Menus can also have *exclusive* or *nonexclusive settings* that users choose to set parameters. In addition, menus can have a pushpin to keep them on the screen for repeated use.

Users can choose from menus using the MENU mouse button in two basic ways:

☐ Press-drag-release

☐ Click-move-click

The most common way to use a menu is by pressing MENU to display the menu, dragging the pointer to the desired item, and releasing the MENU mouse button to choose the item and dismiss the menu. Users must keep the MENU button pressed down to keep the menu on the screen.

Alternatively, users can click MENU once to display the menu and keep it on the screen without holding down the mouse button. Users then move the pointer to the desired item and click either SELECT or MENU again to choose the item and dismiss the menu.

Scrolling Actions

Scrollbars allow users to change the view on the data that is displayed in an application pane. You can describe the detailed actions required to scroll an object, or you can describe scrolling the contents of the pane.

The elements of the scrollbar are described in the Glossary. A summary of parts of the scrollbar is provided here and illustrated in Figure B-5:

☐ *Cable anchors* (top or bottom, left or right)

☐ *Cable*

☐ *Proportion indicator*

☐ *Scrolling arrows (scrolling buttons)*

☐ *Drag area*

☐ *Elevator*

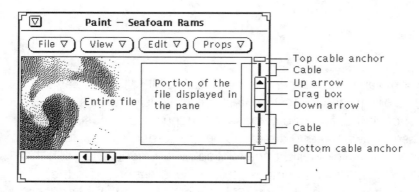

Figure B-5 Names of the elements of a scrollbar.

Figure B-6 shows how users can scroll through the data by manipulating the scrollbar with the SELECT mouse button.

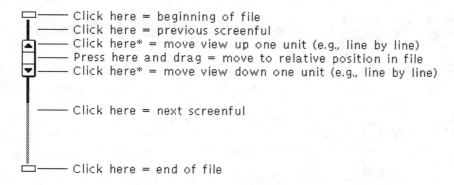

```
☐──── Click here = beginning of file
 │ ──── Click here = previous screenful
 ▲ ──── Click here* = move view up one unit (e.g., line by line)
 │ ──── Press here and drag = move to relative position in file
 ▼ ──── Click here* = move view down one unit (e.g., line by line)


   ──── Click here = next screenful


☐──── Click here = end of file
```

Figure B-6 A functionally annotated scrollbar. Items with an asterisk repeat the action when users press SELECT.

Selecting and Manipulating Objects

Users generally *select* graphic objects, windows, and icons by moving the pointer onto the object and clicking SELECT. Clicking ADJUST *toggles* the state of the selected object, and adds it to the group of selected objects when it is selected.

Text is usually selected by moving the pointer to the correct place, pressing SELECT, *wiping through* or *dragging through* the text to be selected, and releasing SELECT.

Selected objects can be manipulated directly by dragging or by choosing a control from a control area, a menu, or a pop-up window.

Writing Style Guidelines

☑ The term "selection" has a specific and narrowly defined meaning in the OPEN LOOK UI. In the select-then-operate environment, the selection is an object that is chosen so that it can be acted upon.

   Windows, icons, and panes can be selected. Data in panes, such as text and graphic objects, can also be selected.

☑ Be sure to avoid using the term "selection" in conjunction with menu item, buttons, or settings. Controls and menu items are activated, chosen, or invoked (never selected).

☑ Use action verbs to describe the way a user interacts with controls. Instruct users to display menus and pop-up windows, choose settings and items from menus, use buttons, drag slider and scrollbar drag boxes, press or click mouse buttons, and type or enter a value into a text or numeric field.

☑ Use the following terms to describe the usual feedback when a control is activated. Buttons, items on menus, and data in a text field are high-lighted; the border of a chosen setting thickens or is bold; and a check box is checked or unchecked.

☑ When writing for an environment that uses a mouse, always refer to the buttons on the mouse as mouse buttons to avoid confusion with buttons in applications.

☑ Keep users' attention focused on the screen by writing about the pointer, not the mouse.

   Users move the pointer on the screen by moving the mouse.

☑ Make a clear distinction between clicking and pressing, because some actions in the OPEN LOOK UI occur when users push a mouse button down and other, distinct actions occur when users release the mouse button.

☑ Use the following prepositions to describe moving and positioning of the pointer:

  ☑ Move the pointer *into* a control area, menu, pane, or window.
  ☑ Move the pointer *onto* a control or the header of a window.
  ☑ Point *to* a control (same as move onto).
  ☑ Click or press *in* a pane.
  ☑ Click or press *on* a control, region, window, or the workspace.

As a general rule, users can move the pointer into objects that contain other objects (workspace, window, control area). Users can move the pointer onto smaller units that perform specific functions, such as buttons, settings, or the header of a window.

☑ When you first talk about choosing items or settings from a menu, use step-by-step instructions in the following manner:

  1 Move the pointer onto the Edit menu button and press MENU.

  2 Drag the pointer onto the Paste item.

  3 Release MENU. The contents of the clipboard are inserted at the insert point.

☑ After you have explained how things work, you can shortcut the process by saying "Choose Paste from the Edit menu."

Consistency

One of the goals of the OPEN LOOK UI design is to promote consistency among applications. Consistent use of OPEN LOOK UI terminology can do a great deal to convince users that OPEN LOOK UI applications are consistent. Technical writers and editors appreciate style guides and terminology lists.

☑ Encourage those who write about your applications to adopt and use the correct terminology to further the consistency of applications developed using the OPEN LOOK user interface.

GLOSSARY

Abbreviated button 	A button that is displayed as a small square with a glyph inside the border. Abbreviated buttons function just like buttons.
Abbreviated menu button 	A menu button that is displayed as a small square with a hollow triangle inside the border. The triangle points downward when the menu is displayed below the menu button, and to the right when the menu is displayed to the right. The current setting is usually displayed to the right of the abbreviated menu button. Abbreviated menu buttons function just like menu buttons.
ADJUST mouse button	The mouse button that is used to adjust (extend or reduce) the selection.
Apply (Apply)	Executes the property window settings affecting the selection.

Automatic scrolling	When not all of a file is visible in a window, the view in a pane automatically shifts to follow the movement of the pointer as users press SELECT and wipe through the data.
Background	An underlying area on which objects, such as controls and windows, are displayed.
Base window	The primary window for an application.

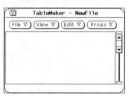

Basic pointer	An arrow pointing northeast that shows the mouse position on the workspace.
Blocking	A window that does not allow input to any other window of the application except itself.
Bounding box	A rectangle that is displayed on the screen to define a region for selection.
Busy pattern	A standard pattern displayed in the header of a window or within the border of a button to show that the application is temporarily performing a function and cannot accept input.
Busy pointer	The pointer that is displayed by the system when an application is busy and cannot accept input at the pointer location.

Button	A one-choice element of a control area or a menu. Buttons are used to execute commands (command button), display pop-up windows (window button), and to display menus (menu button).
Button menu	A menu that is displayed when the pointer is on a menu button and users press MENU.
Cable	The scrollbar cable represents the total size of the data that users can view in the pane. The elevator moves up and down the cable to show the position of the view into the data.
Cable anchor	The buttons at the ends of the scrollbar cable.
Caret	Windows that accept keyboard input display a caret to show the insert point. An active caret is a solid triangle that may blink. An inactive caret is a dimmed diamond.
Categories	Groups of like settings in a Property window.
Change bars 	Vertical lines on the left side of Property window panes that show that a setting has been modified but not applied. In some implementations, change bars can be dimmed to show changes that have been made but not yet applied.

Check boxes

A nonexclusive setting that shows a check mark in a square box when the setting is chosen.

Click

To press a mouse button once and release it without moving the pointer beyond the damping factor.

Clipboard

The means for keeping track of data that is cut or copied. The Paste key is used to insert information from the clipboard into a pane. Also, an item on the Workspace Utilities submenu that displays a window showing the contents of the clipboard.

Command button

(**Print**)

A button that is used to execute application commands (see Button).

Command item

Print

An item on a menu or submenu that is used to execute application commands.

Command window

A pop-up window that is used to execute application commands or set parameters.

Completion message

A status message in the footer of a window.

Control area

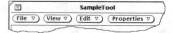

An unbordered region of a window where controls such as buttons, settings, and text fields are displayed.

Controls

Objects in a control area, a pane, or on a menu that are used to perform an action. Controls include buttons, items on menus, exclusive and nonexclusive settings, sliders, gauges, text fields, and check boxes.

Copy

To duplicate selected text or graphics onto the clipboard.

Core functions

Essential functions that are always available from the keyboard. These functions can also be provided on buttons in control areas or on menus.

Current item

An active item in a scrolling list.

| Courier |

Cut

To remove selected objects from a window and store them on the clipboard.

Damping factor

The number of pixels users can move the pointer before a drag is initiated.

Default

The assumed setting for a menu that users can change. Also the specified button in a pop-up window that is activated by the Default Action key on the keyboard.

Default ring

The default button in a pop-up window, which has a ring displayed inside the button border. The default item on a menu or submenu has a 1-point ring around the item when an item is not highlighted.

Dimmed controls

An inactive control is dimmed to show that it cannot accept input from the mouse or the keyboard.

Direct manipulation

To move or copy a selected object by dragging it.

Double-click

Clicking twice on a mouse button as an accelerator that performs a specific function without using a menu.

Drag

To press and hold down any mouse button while moving the pointer—and the object under the pointer—on the screen.

Drag Area

The area in the middle of the scrollbar elevator or slider.

Dragging Modifiers

Keys on the keyboard that, when pressed in conjunction with a mouse button, modify dragging actions.

Duplicate pointer

The pointer that is displayed when users copy an object by dragging.

Elevator

The part of the scrollbar that has up and down arrows and a drag area. The elevator rides the scrollbar cable and shows the position of the view in the pane relative to the total data available.

Embedded objects

Objects that are nested in other containers, typically frames, either of the same or a different type.

End boxes

Small rectangular buttons on a slider that are used to set the minimum or maximum setting.

Exclusive Scrolling List

A scrolling list from which users can choose only one item at a given time.

Exclusive setting

A control that is used for mutually exclusive settings and that is identified by touching rectangles. The chosen setting is shown with a bold border around it.

File Manager

The file management application used in an OPEN LOOK UI implementation to load, store, and browse through files from the workspace and from within an application.

Footer

The bottom area of a window. The footer is used by an application for information and error messages.

Foreground

The controls and the pane of a window.

Frames

Bordered screen regions (or object containers) that can contain application-specific objects. Borders are not necessarily visible.

Full Size

To increase the size of a window to its maximum as determined by the application. Full Size is an item on the Window menu that allows users to perform that function. After users make a window full size, the label in the item toggles to Restore Size.

Gauge

A read-only control that shows the percent of use or the portion of an action that has been completed.

Glyph

A picture or graphic representation of an object.

Grab handles

The small squares that are displayed at the corners and midpoints of the region that defines a selected graphic object.

Halation

The "glowing" effect of screen elements giving off light.

Header

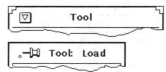

The band across the top of every window. Each header has a centered title. Base windows have a Window menu button on the left; pop-up windows have a pushpin on the left.

Help

An OPEN LOOK UI implementation provides on-screen help for each element in a window. The application provides help for application functions and elements. The Help function must be available from the keyboard.

Hierarchical scrolling list

A multi-level scrolling list in which items can be categorized and embedded within one another.

Highlighting

A visual indication that an object is in a special state. In monochrome implementations, the visual indication is reverse video. In color implementations, users can set the selection highlighting color.

Hot spot	The place on the pointer that determines the exact spot on the screen where an action is performed.
Icon	A small pictorial representation of a base window. Displaying objects as icons conserves screen real estate while keeping the window available for easy access.

Image	A picture or graphic representation of an object.
Inactive feedback	An inactive control that is dimmed cannot accept input from the mouse or the keyboard.

Indeterminate state

Size: [Small | Medium | Large]

A control has a dimmed border to indicate that an application cannot clearly show all the attributes of a selected object. The label and control names are not dimmed.

Indexed help

A feature of the Help window that displays help information by topic.

Input area

The place on the screen that accepts keyboard input. Click SELECT to set the insert point in the input area (click-to-type).

Insert point

▲

The specific location in the input area where keyboard input is displayed. When users set the insert point, an active caret is displayed.

Instruction messages	Prompting messages that inform users of the next logical step.
Intention-based	A control area in which controls are based on categories of user actions versus types of objects in the application (see Object-based).
Items	Menu controls that initiate actions. Also, choices found in a scrolling list.
Keyboard	Commonly used alphanumeric input device.
Keyboard accelerator	A key or sequence of keys on the keyboard, or multiple clicks of mouse buttons, through which users can quickly perform specific menu or application functions without using a menu.
Keyboard equivalent	A specific default key sequence that provides functionality without requiring the display of a menu.
Label	The title of a button, item, or setting that describes its function.
Layer	Windows and icons that overlap one another on the workspace.

Levels	Different parts of a hierarchical structure that can be accessed in a scrolling list. Also different certification levels for an OPEN LOOK toolkit. A Level 1 toolkit contains the basic elements for the OPEN LOOK UI. A Level 2 toolkit contains a complete set of elements. Level 3 toolkits provide additional, expanded functionality.

Long-term message

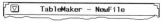

Text that is displayed in a window header following the window title and two hyphens or a single em-dash.

Menu

A rectangle containing a group of controls. Menus are displayed in two ways: from a menu button with choices appropriate to the menu button label (button menu) and from any place on the screen that is not a control (pop-up menu). The pop-up menu displays choices appropriate to the pointer location.

Menu button

(**Menu Button** ▽)

A multiple-choice control. A menu button always has a menu mark and is used to display a menu.

Menu group

A menu and its associated submenus.

Menu item

Menu Item ▷

An item on a menu with a menu mark pointing to the right that is used to display a submenu.

Menu mark

▽ ▷

A hollow triangle in the border of a button or following a menu item that has a submenu attached to it. The triangle points to where the menu or submenu is displayed.

MENU mouse button	The mouse button that is used to display menus.
Message	Information generated by an application that informs users about the status of a process.
Message log	A history of status messages.
Mnemonic key	A key that represents the first letter of a command and is thus easy to remember. It is generally used in conjunction with a modifier, such as Control or Shift, as a keyboard accelerator. For example, Control-P could mean Print.
More button (More)	A button an application can add to its Help window to allow users to access other types of on-line help, such as on-line documentation.
Mouse	An electronic or mechanical device that is used to select and manipulate information on a computer screen.
Move	To remove selected text or graphics from a window and put it on the clipboard. Also, to change the location of selected text, graphics, windows, or icons by dragging to a new location.
Move pointer	The pointer that is displayed when users move an object by dragging.
Multi-click	Clicking a mouse button rapidly a specific number of times. Multiclicking is usually an accelerator for functions that can be accessed in other ways.
Nonexclusive scrolling list	A scrolling list from which users can choose one or more items at a given time.

Nonexclusive setting

A list of nonexclusive choices indicated by separated rectangles. The chosen settings are surrounded by a bold border.

Normalization

Moving scrolled objects in discrete units so that a defined unit is always visible in the pane. For example, normalized text scrolls line by line. Characters in a line are never chopped in half.

Notice

Window that is displayed when an application generates warning and error messages that require an action before users can proceed. Notices block input to the application until users click on one of its buttons.

Numeric field

Point Size: 12 ▲▼

Text input field with increment and decrement buttons that is used for numeric input.

Object-based

A control area in which controls are based on types of objects in the application rather than on user actions (see Intention-based).

OPEN LOOK™

A trademark of AT&T.

Page-oriented scrollbar

A scrollbar with a box that shows the current page number when users press SELECT on the drag area of the elevator. The box expands and contracts to the left to accommodate different numbers of digits.

Palette

A set of coordinated colors provided for defining the color of the workspace, window background, selection, and caret.

Pane

A bordered rectangle in a window where the application displays its data.

Panning

A method of scrolling in which users directly drag the contents of the pane instead of using the scrollbar.

Panning pointer

The pointer that is displayed when users initiate panning. The point of the arrow is the hot spot.

Paste

To insert data from the clipboard into a window. Selected data is placed on the clipboard with the COPY or CUT key.

Pinned menu

A menu that has its pushpin pushed in. A pinned menu is a pop-up window and remains on the workspace until users dismiss it.

Pixel

An abbreviation for picture element, the smallest unit that can be displayed on a computer screen.

Pointer

Any graphic representation of the location of the mouse on the screen. *See also* Basic pointer, Busy pointer, Duplicate pointer, Move pointer, Panning pointer, Text duplicate pointer, and Text move pointer.

Pointer jumping	When the pointer automatically moves to a specific location, such as to a Notice or a pop-up window.
Pointing device	A mechanical or electronic device used to manipulate the screen pointer.

Pop-up menu

A menu that users access by pressing MENU on any area of the workspace that is not a control. The menu that is displayed depends on the location of the mouse pointer.

Pop-up window

A window that pops up to perform a specific function and that is then dismissed. Command windows, Property windows, Help windows and Notices are all pop-up windows.

Pop-up Window menu

The Window menu that is displayed when users press MENU on the background of a pop-up window.

Press	To push and hold a mouse button.
Progress message	Information generated by an application that informs users about the status of a process.
Properties	Characteristics of an object that users can set, such as the color of a window.
PROPERTIES	A Level 1 core function that is used to display a Property window for the selected object.

Property window

A pop-up window that is used to set properties associated with an object, an application, or a window.

Proportion indicator

The dark area of the scrollbar cable showing the proportion of data that is currently viewed in the pane, relative to the total length of the cable. The cable represents the total size of the data.

Pushpin

A glyph that can be used to keep a menu, Property window, or command window displayed on the screen.

Question mark pointer

?

The pointer that is displayed when users click or press a mouse button and the window manager cannot perform an action. This pointer is also displayed if users drag an object to an inappropriate destination.

Quick duplicate

A means of copying text without changing the existing text selection.

Quick move

A means of moving text without changing the existing text selection.

Release

To stop pressing a mouse button.

Reset

(Reset)

Restores the property window controls to their previous state.

Resize corner

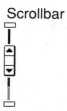

Areas that provide an unconstrained resizing of the boundaries of the window, without changing the scale of the contents of the window. Only windows that can be resized have resize corners.

Resize handles

Handles on the sides of a pane that can be adjusted; they are displayed when users select the pane.

Scale

To make everything in the window bigger or smaller while keeping all elements of the window proportional to one another and the contents anchored at the upper left corner. Users choose the scale for base or pop-up windows from the application Property window.

Scrollbar

A control that is used to move the view of the data displayed in the pane.

Scrollbar menu

A pop-up menu associated with each scrollbar that is used to reposition the data in the pane.

Scrolling

Moving through data that cannot be viewed entirely in a pane.

Scrolling button

An abbreviated button with a solid triangular arrowhead inside the border that is used for scrolling.

Scrolling list

Font:
| Avante Garde |
| Courier |
| Gothic |
| Helvetica |
| Modern |

A pane containing a list of text fields. The list can be read-only or it can be editable.

Select

To distinguish an object (or objects) on the screen so that they can be operated on.

SELECT mouse button

The mouse button that is used to select objects, set the insert point, manipulate controls, and drag objects.

Select-then-operate paradigm

Selecting an object and then choosing an operation from a menu (or the keyboard) to perform an action on the selected object(s). The object (or objects) for selection can be text or graphics within an application, a pane, a window, or an icon.

Settings

| Draw | Paint |

| Bold | | Italic | | Underscore |

Controls for choosing predetermined values.

Short-term message

Text that is displayed in the left portion of a window footer, usually displaying instructions, progress, or error messages.

Shrink

To resize a window so that its area is reduced.

Slider

A control used to set a value and give a visual indication of the setting.

Smart word handling

The correct handling of white space on either side of text that is moved or duplicated.

Split

To divide a pane into parts using the cable anchors of the scrollbar.

Spot help

A brief message pertaining to the object under the pointer when users press the Help key.

Status message

Information generated by an application that informs users about the progress of a process.

Submenu

A menu that displays additional choices under a menu item on a menu.

Table

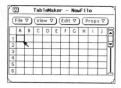

A display of data in rows and columns.

Target pointer

The halo that is displayed around the hot spot of the basic pointer when the pointer is on the border of a narrow or small object.

Text duplicate pointer

The pointer that is displayed when users are duplicating text directly by dragging.

Text field **File Name:** <u>Doc1</u>	An area in a window into which users type text from the keyboard.
Text move pointer <u>The</u> ▸	The pointer that is displayed when users are moving text directly by dragging.
Text region	A multi-line area in a window into which users type text from the keyboard.
Title [Text]	The name of the application or function that is displayed at the top of a window or a pop-up menu.
Toolkit	A set of programming components used to build applications.
Undo	To return an object to its state before users performed the last operation. Levels of undo are determined by the application.
Validate	To have the application verify that the contents of a text field are appropriate to the function.
Window	A rectangle containing application elements.

Window background	The area outside any panes, including the header, footer, and sides of the window.

Window button

A button that is used to display a window containing additional controls.

Window item
Window Item...

An item on a menu that is used to display a window containing additional controls.

Window mark

The three dots (...) that are displayed following the button label on window buttons, and following a window item on a menu.

Window menu

The menu that is accessed from the background of a window. Pop-up windows have a window menu with slightly different choices than those of the base window menu.

Window menu button

The abbreviated menu button that is always displayed at the left of the header in each base window that can be used to execute the default setting on the Window menu (by clicking SELECT) and to display the Window menu (by pressing MENU).

Workspace

The background screen area on which windows and icons are displayed.

Workspace menu

The menu that controls global functions.

Workspace Properties
window

The Property window accessed from the Workspace menu that allows users to customize your
workspace environment.

References

General

Brown, C. M., *Human–Computer Interface Design Guidelines,* Ablex Publishing, 1988.

Davis, E. and R. Swezey, "Human Factors Guidelines in Computer Graphics, a Case Study," *International Journal of Man–Machine Studies,* Vol 18, 1983, pp. 113–133.

Reilly, S. and J. Roach, "Improved Visual Design for Graphics Display," *IEEE Computer Graphics and Applications,* Vol 4, No 2, February 1984, pp. 42–51.

Shneiderman, B., *Designing the User Interface: Strategies for Effective Human–Computer Interaction,* Addison-Wesley, 1987.

Sun Microsystems, Inc., *OPEN LOOK Graphical User Interface Functional Specification,* Addison-Wesley, 1989.

Color

Christ, R., "Review and Analysis of Color Coding Research for Visual Displays," *Human Factors,* Vol. 17, 1975, pp. 542–570.

Christ, R. and M. Corso, "Color Research for Visual Displays," ONR report No ONR–CR213–102–3, NTIS AD No A031105, July 1975.

Frome, F., "Improving Color CAD Systems for Users: Some Suggestions from Human Factors Studies," *IEEE Design and Test of Computers,* Vol 1, No 1, February 1984, pp. 18–27.

Krebs, M., J. Wolf, and J. Sandvig, "Color Display Design Guide," ONR Report No ONR–CR213–136–2F, NTIS AD No A066630, October 1978.

Murch, G., "Physiological Principles for the Effective Use of Color," *IEEE Computer Graphics and Applications,* Vol 4, No 11, November 1984, pp. 49–54.

— "The Effective Use of Color: Cognitive Principles," *TEKniques,* Vol 8, No 2, Summer 1984, pp. 25–31.

— "The Effective Use of Color: Perceptual Principles" *TEKniques,* Vol 8, No 1, Spring 1984, pp. 4–9.

— "The Effective Use of Color: Physiological Principles," *TEKniques,* Vol 7, No 4, Winter 1984, pp. 13–16.

Teichner, W., R. Christ, and G. Corso, "Color Research for Visual Displays," ONR Report No ONR–CR213–102–4F, NTIS AD No A043609, June 1977.

INDEX

A

Abbreviated menu button (s), *54*, 210–*11*
 cycling through options with, 271, *272*
 grouping, 268–69
 labeling, 254
 scrolling lists used with, 273–74
 text fields used with, 273
Accelerators (*see* Keyboard accelerators)
Action (s), 2
 application-specific, 23, 27–28
 completion/incompletion messages, 307–9
 design issues and, 19
 linking objects with specific, 31–33
 stop, 183
Active caret, 343
ADJUST function, 43, 342
Again command (Edit menu), 26, 204

Application (s)
 accessing other parts of, 98–99
 design principles, 1–9
  coexistence, 8–9
  consistency, 4–6
  efficiency, 6–8
  simplicity, 2–4
 diagramming functionality of, 99
 structure, 11–35
  base windows, 17–22
  command windows, 31–34
  general considerations, 12–13
  icons, 13–17
  objects and properties, 29–31
  window control-area menu buttons, 22–28
 titles of, *239, 304*
Apply button, *89*, 112, *113*, 149, *150*
Automatic scrolling, 162–63

I

Icon (s), 38, 339, *340*
  base window, 67, 71
  busy, *226*
  characteristics of workspace, 47–48
  color used in, 321
  design issues, 13–17
    consolidating representation, 15
    indicating progress and completion, 16–17
    representing data files and other objects, 14–15
    representing multiple functions, 15
    representing processes, 14
    representing related applications, 15–16
  error message for, 301
  feedback for selection of, *171*
  positioning on the grid, 48, 237, 248
  receiving dropped data on, 164–65
  standard vs. nonstandard, *238*
  titles and glyphs for, 237–41
Import command (File menu), 24
Inactive controls
  feedback for, 159–60, 226–28, 343
  help for, 135, *136*
Indeterminate feedback, 228–29
Indexed help, 132, *133*
Input. *See also* Data, selecting
  design issues, 23–24
  keyboard, 45–46, 181–89
  validating, 230, 311–12
Input area, 47, 341, 343
Insert item (Scrolling List menu), 220
Insert point, 46, 343
Instruction messages, 309–*10*
Intention-based approach in applications vs. object-based approach, 209–10
Items (*see* Menu items)

J

Joining panes, 80, 84–85
Join Views (Scrollbar menu), 80, 85

K

Keyboard, 181–89
  active area for input by, 47
  core functions, 45–46, 181–84
    cut/copy/paste, 182
    help, 183
    properties, 183
    stop, 183
    undo, 183–84
  designing for best usage of, 4–5
  dragging operations, 184–86
    constrain, 185
    duplicate, 185–86
    keyboard mappings, 184–85
    panning, 186
    Set Menu default, 185
  equivalents, 8
  miscellaneous functions, 46
  mouse modifiers, 45
Keyboard accelerators, 8, 186–89
  mnemonic keys vs. function keys, 187
  modifier keys, 187–88
  numbered, 189
  user mapping of, 186–87

L

Label (s), 3, 235, 250, 251–63
  for abbreviated menus, 254
  characteristics, 252
  for check boxes, 255
  combining titles and, 261–63

N

O